"Enjoy and adolescence are two words that should go together."

*You Can Enjoy Your Teen* shows you how these two seemingly unrelated words can be synchronized to make your household a place abounding in joy and harmony.

Dr. Jim Geddes offers a basic formula that will guide you toward delighting in your teen:

If you love and understand them
and teach them
and accept them
and confront them,
and release them,
you will enjoy your teenager.

He takes you through steps to implement this within your family. While addressing the inevitable problems that must be faced, Dr. Geddes emphasizes the opportunities they offer for turning bad situations into good ones. No matter how skeptical you may be, let this encouraging and informative book prove that you *can* enjoy your teen...*frequently!*

# You Can Enjoy Your Teen

# You *Can* Enjoy Your Teen

## DR. JIM GEDDES

**Power Books**

Fleming H. Revell
Old Tappan, New Jersey

Unless otherwise indicated, Scripture quotations in this volume are taken from the King James Version of the Bible.

Scripture quotations identified NEB are from The New English Bible. Copyright © The Delegates of the Oxford University Press and the Syndics of the Cambridge University Press 1961, 1970. Reprinted by permission.

Verses marked TLB are taken from The Living Bible, Copyright © 1971 by Tyndale House Publishers, Wheaton, Ill. Used by permission.

Library of Congress Cataloging-in-Publication Data
Geddes, Jim.
    You can enjoy your teen / Jim Geddes.
        p.      cm.
    ISBN 0-8007-5292-9
    1. Teenagers.   2. Adolescent psychology.   3. Parenting.
I. Title.
HQ796.G36 1989                                    88-30211
305.2'35—dc19                                          CIP

Copyright © 1989 by Jim Geddes
Published by the Fleming H. Revell Company
Old Tappan, New Jersey 07675
Printed in the United States of America

# Contents

## Part I
### Teenagers Are Great!

## Part II
### Understand Them

## Part III
### Help Your Adolescents

## Part IV
### Enjoy Them

# Preface

The teen years should be an enjoyable experience for both parents and their maturing children. God intends your household to be a place where you and your teenagers can enjoy your final years together and then part as friends.

If you are not enjoying your teen, or if you would like to enjoy him or her more, this book challenges you to *enjoy by understanding*. That is, *understand* your adolescent by carefully considering the development process underway in each of the three sub-stages of adolescence:

- *early adolescence*—searching for identity
- *middle adolescence*—breaking the emotional tie to parents
- *later adolescence*—pursuing love and meaningful, significant work

This book also challenges you to *enjoy by helping*. You will *enjoy* your teenager as you *help* her to let go of childhood, as you stop treating him like a child. This book seeks to strengthen your skills in *teaching, accepting, loving, confronting,* and *releasing,* because your mastery of these skills will help your teens to enjoy their adolescence and will help you to enjoy them.

UNDERSTANDING plus HELPING leads to ENJOYMENT.

Accept the challenge to *understand*.

Accept the challenge to *help appropriately*.

Then you will *enjoy* your adolescent!

# Ten Commandments for Enjoying Your Teen

    I.   Welcome adolescence and its constant changes as part of God's perfect, creative work.

    II.   Realize that your teenager is neither child nor adult, but a special kind of person in a unique period of life.

    III.   Encourage your early teen in his search for an identity that is personal, unique, and different from that of either parent.

    IV.   Don't be an obstacle to your middle teen's efforts to break the tie of emotional dependence on parents.

    V.   Affirm your later teen's desire to seek love and companionship with opposite-sexed peers.

    VI.   Reinforce your later teen's interest in meaningful work, which will balance out the strong desire for love.

    VII.   Take a stand with your teen on family values, sex, alcohol, and drugs; teach your teen to treat you with respect.

    VIII.   Accept and love your teenager, but balance acceptance with appropriate rejection.

    IX.   Confront your teenager about every aspect of the relationship that you consider to be unfair.

    X.   Release your teen gradually and graciously to full freedom and responsibility.

# PART ONE

## Teenagers Are Great!

# 1

## God's Perfect, Creative Work Is Unfolding

They stood there an arm's length apart, a short mother and her tall, 16-year-old son. They glared at each other, he looking down and she looking up at this tall string of unthinking, impractical, overconfident humanity. Will he ever grow up and be responsible? she wondered to herself. Will she ever let me be responsible to run my own life? he wondered to himself.

They were both tired of yelling, and Mom deftly defused the situation by saying, "I could clobber you, but I would only hurt my hand on your big bones!" (He grinned.) "Let's call a ten-minute truce, and I will wash my face and cool off. Why don't you make us a pot of coffee? Then we'll sit down and see where we are. Maybe after a short break, we can work something out." "Okay, Mom," he replied, and walked to the kitchen.

Sure enough, reason soon began to prevail, and mother and son were able to sit down and work through some of their problems. They were problems similar to those faced by adolescents and their parents everywhere:

- *his wants* (he wants a larger and larger share of the family's resources, including money, the car, expensive clothes, Mom's time and energy for a thousand things, and his own freedom and independence).
- *his parents' wants* (they want the wages from his part-time employment to cover more of his basic needs, and they want a growing percentage of their money, time, and energy to be directed to their own pursuits).
- *his parents' demands* (they demand that he accept the household rules while he is living under their roof, and they demand to be treated with courtesy, respect, and appreciation).

Fortunately, he has said often over the years, "I love you, Mom, you know I love you," and his words have helped to heal many wounds. Fortunately too, they both know about compromise, and they are learning not to be too harsh or stubborn. They know the importance of meeting each other halfway. And fortunately, Mom knows that God is in her son's resistance to her control. She knows that God's perfect, creative work is unfolding in her son's growth and development away from her household and away from her control. It is time to loosen her grip, to let go further, and further, and further . . . but oh, how she loves him!

## God Is the Author of Adolescence

What is your attitude toward adolescents with all of their illusions, excesses, and imbalances? Do you understand that God's creative work is ongoing within them? Yes, He created the world long ago, but *He is still creating;* and adolescence, just as much as conception, pregnancy, infancy, and childhood, is part of His beautiful, ongoing, unfolding, creative work.

*Adolescence is not a mistake—it is a perfection!* It is an exact and perfect stage of growth and development that is the period of changing from child to adult. The very features of adolescence that are so frustrating to parents and adolescents themselves—adolescent illusions of greatness, the adolescent preoccupation with freedom and independence—these features are the way they are because the Great Creator, in His infinite wisdom and unlimited power, has designed adolescence as an ideal, final preparation for adulthood. Put in the strongest terms, every biological and psychological feature of adolescence is part of God's design. It is a perfect means to bring the adolescent to full adulthood.

## What Are the Facts?

The first fact is frustrating: the human genitals mature ten years before the human brain finishes its maturing process! This means that healthy, strong, sexually mature adolescent males and females still do not have certain connective tissues of the brain functioning at full efficiency. Adolescents can think, yes, and they can learn, remember, and problem-solve, but the connectors between their thinking centers (the cerebral cortex) and their emotions (the hypothalamus) are not yet fully operational. This biological fact of adolescence raises the question, Why is there this puzzling ten-year delay in brain development? There is a good answer to this question. It has to do with the breaking of the tie of emotional dependence between adolescents and their parents.

Human young are intensely attached to their parents, and human parents are also intensely attached to their young. Breaking down this emotional dependence is a primary goal of adolescence, and this detachment process is accomplished partly by the illusions of greatness and superiority common among adolescents. Kyle, age 14, imagines that he is quite superior in knowledge and wisdom to both of his parents. This illusion of personal greatness gives him courage to oppose his parents' reasoning and to fashion goals and an identity of his own. Kyle has no idea that his courage, overconfidence, and abounding self-esteem—and his critical attitude toward others—are fostered by his high blood plasma level of the sex hormone testosterone. This very high hormonal level, which is a normal level for Kyle's age, is God's way of helping Kyle to develop his own identity and to get the courage eventually to leave home. Years later, when Kyle is living independently (and his hormonal level has dropped dramatically!), the illusions of his greatness will end. Kyle may find himself saying, with Mark Twain:

> *"When I was a boy of fourteen, my*
> *father was so ignorant I could*
> *hardly stand to have the old man*
> *around. But when I got to be twenty-one*
> *I was astonished at how much*
> *he had learnt in seven years."*

The next fact is an encouraging one. Most males experience, at age 19½, a 50 percent drop in their blood plasma levels of testosterone. This reduction, occurring over a six-month period, results in dramatic behavioral changes, helping most males of this age to recover their common sense and rejoin the human race. No wonder Mark Twain saw things differently at age 21: his hormonal drop had helped him to get a better perspective. Many parents of rebellious 18-year-olds who hang their heads in shame are quite proud of those same sons at age 21, and even take credit for their maturity and improvement! Little do they know how much the change was due to the testosterone drop and also due to the increased efficiency of the limbic connectors in the brain.

So there is hope for all young people! This is not a time for parents to despair—it is a time to hang in there—to love, to understand, to accept, to confront, to release, to enjoy their adolescents. God is doing His creative work in our conception, our birth, infancy, and childhood. But He doesn't stop at childhood. His hand is at the helm of adolescence too, and He controls our growth, our hormone levels, our brain development, and everything else. God is the author of adolescence—let every parent and every teenager take heart.

In the chapters ahead, we will study every major aspect of adolescent psychological development and how parents and teens can make the best of this beautiful stage of human maturation. We shall see that teenagers are great, *because God is with them and He is guiding their development.*

It's not that adolescents are greater than the rest of us. Some cultures are worshiping at the altar of youth, and they appear to be so entranced with adolescent vitality, adolescent illusions, and adolescent thinking that there is a danger of becoming a teenage-dominated society. Let us not be fooled: adolescence is only a step along the way; it is not the goal. The goal is a person with maturity, balance, and a clear sense of reality that is quite beyond the average teen. Adults need to enjoy the freshness and vitality of teenagers, without forgetting that teens still have a long way to go. Adolescents should be made fully responsible for their own actions, but they are a long way from being ready to take over the world!

## Adolescence Is a Psychological Wonder

Crystal, age 13, is already as tall as her mother, and as intelligent. She does not think very logically yet, but the growth in her thinking ability is rapid. She is now able, for the first time in her life, to think about her own thinking and to think about the thinking of others. Crystal spends a lot of time daydreaming (as her mother calls it), and during her daydreaming she is thinking of what others are thinking of her. This is the main psychological feature of adolescence. It centers around the question, *"What are others thinking about me?"* It is a valuable exercise, and from it

Crystal is gaining a strengthened sense of her identity—who she is and how she may want to change and improve.

However, Crystal is suffering from an illusion—a false view of things. She imagines that others are thinking about her constantly, and that they are as preoccupied with her behavior, attitudes, and interests as she is. This causes her to believe that she is the center of interest and attention wherever she goes. She says to herself, if she is on center stage, then shouldn't she act and perform for her audience? "Everyone is noticing my hairstyle, clothing, complexion, figure, my conversation, my wit, my charm, and I mustn't disappoint them." Crystal works hard to give her best appearance and performance for the imaginary audience.

Crystal and her mother get along fairly well, but they do have their verbal battles at times. Crystal is growing toward the time when the opinions of her peers, her own generation, are very important to her, and Mother's opinions are becoming less so. This is natural and normal for Crystal, because her very nature and her instincts and intuitions are causing her to choose to make her future with her own generation. She is not so much rebelling against her parents as she is resisting their influence in a powerful attempt to be in tune with her peers. This is a process of *reverse identification*, and it means she unconsciously reaches out to consider and evaluate those beliefs, attitudes, and life-styles that are *different* from those of her parents. At ages 2 and 3 she did the opposite, that is, she identified with her parents, and this meant that she unthinkingly accepted her parents' beliefs, attitudes, and life-style. But in adolescence Crystal seeks her own identity by considering many different sets of values and life-styles. She may or may not end up accepting as her own the values and life-style of her parents at the end of her teen years, but first she must consider the alternatives. Many of the terrible battles between adolescents and their parents are rooted in the teen's determination to identify with peers and to reverse identify, or resist, the values and life-style of parents.

Crystal has another illusion, or false view of things, that is a necessary part of adolescent thinking. She imagines that she is absolutely unique, different, and special, and that all the rest—even her peers!—are experiencing life and individuality on a lesser level. "No one ever before has experienced such intense pleasure and sheer ecstasy as I have." "No one ever before has suffered as I have suffered." "No one has figured out the great questions of life as well as I have." "No one is as handsome (or strong or clever) as I am." While much of this thinking is an error and illusion (sometimes referred to as the *personal fable*), yet it serves the wholesome purpose *temporarily* of building up a sense of identity, self-confidence, and self-esteem, which together can be a good basis for mental health in adult life.

Crystal's mother is surprised and amazed that Crystal, with her illusions, excesses, and resistances, is nevertheless stumbling forward in definite growth and progress. It is all a wonder as it comes together in a new, independent, somewhat immature adult human being. Mother is often frustrated, but she is often proud too. As the years rush by, it is clear that Crystal is becoming an adult, and childhood is slowly but surely being left behind.

But the best of adolescence—middle and later adolescence—is yet to be for Crystal, and that means coming to enjoy the company of opposite-sexed peers in a relaxed, comfortable, and confident way. Adolescence is what is known by psychologists as a *critical period*—a period of time in which certain critical learning ought to take place. In this case, it is *learning to enjoy the company of the opposite-sexed peers.*

Adolescence is not a time for sexual intercourse, but it is the ideal time to begin to socialize with the opposite sex (Crystal is already on the phone each day, talking to girlfriends and interested boys) and to gain confidence in one's ability to enjoy and understand opposite-sexed peers. Ideally, Crystal will have many sporting, church, and social events to attend in which teens of both sexes enjoy one another's company under appropriate supervision. Adulthood is too late for this critical learning to take place, and if this learning is delayed, it only occurs later with greater difficulty.

Last but not least, the psychological development of adolescence depends on the teenager finding *meaningful, productive work.* Teens need to feel that they are capable of contributing to their own survival and that of their family, church, and community. Meaningful, productive work is the finest way for them to gain confidence in their capability to contribute. Adolescents need to work; they need gainful employment. Teens should be working and contributing, at least on a part-time or casual labor basis. You learn to be a giver by giving, and adolescents need this opportunity to give through work. Schoolwork helps a great deal in this direction for those students who really work at their studies. Other teenagers work hard at sports, making a meaningful contribution to their team's success. Music studies are also honorable work, as are other types of art. Volunteer service is also valuable. But employment or part-time employment in meaningful, productive work goes a long way to give adolescents the sense of self-worth and achievement they so desire.

Many of the problems of youth can be traced to problems in this area. One such common problem is the current adolescent overemphasis on sex, which is stimulated by the media and false sexual values. Parents who want to counterbalance this emphasis should use productive work as the counterbalance.

Ed and Sherry are on the right track when they encourage their 16-year-old son Mike to continue his part-time employment of fifteen hours weekly. Not only does Mike get self-respect from paying for many major expenses out of his own earnings, but he also gets the message that life is more than just driving around with his girlfriend. Mike's life has more balance because of his employment; work acts as a counterbalance to the intense but natural and normal interest in sex.

We have looked in the briefest possible way at five psychological features of adolescence: the illusions of the imaginary audience and the personal fable, the critical learning of confidence with opposite-sexed peers, reverse identification, and the importance of meaningful, productive work. We shall look at these in much greater detail in later chapters, but this brief introduction is intended to demonstrate that adolescence is challenging and a wonder to behold. God intends that parents who understand and hold the line should enjoy their teenage children. *Are you enjoying your adolescent?* What changes do you need to make in order to enjoy him or her more?

## Adolescence Is a Biological Unfolding

The bud of the rose unfolds, petal by petal, into full flowering. Then, so briefly, the blossoms stand and dazzle the beholder. All of life is a rapid, unstoppable unfolding, and the blossoms soon fade and fall.

With the same unstoppable unfolding, the human child has been climbing upward through the quiet years of ages 8, 9, and 10, unaware that the biggest changes of life are just ahead. In the diagrams on page 22, notice that age 10 for girls and age 12 for boys are the slowest growth years of all of childhood and adolescence. Then notice the incredible spurt of growth at puberty.

These are height charts, and they reveal several important points that help us understand the biology of adolescence:

1. Females, on average, experience their growth spurt *two full years ahead* of males.
2. Males grow faster than females during the growth spurt, and in

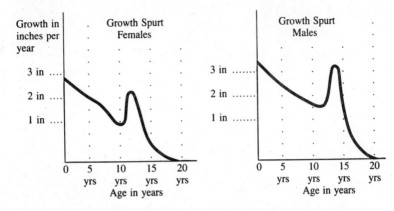

their fourteenth year are growing at an incredible yearly rate of over three inches.

3. The growth spurts of normal adolescents may occur *two full years earlier* than the graphs indicate, or *five years later,* and are still considered to be completely normal. Do not be concerned if puberty comes a little earlier or later than average.

4. Females usually attain their full height by age 14, and males usually attain their full height by age 16.

5. These diagrams portray growth in height only, but the growth of girth and width continues rapidly to the late teens and early twenties. Body mass, in males especially, continues to increase for at least five years after height has been attained in a majority of males. During this period, shoulders, chests, arms continue to increase in size. Females experience an increase in hip size during this later growth phase.

6. The growth of height and girth is stimulated by genetic and hormonal factors, but is also strongly influenced by diet, exercise, rest, and a general sense of well-being.

The great biological unfolding of adolescence all begins with the pineal gland at the base of the brain. The pineal gland begins to decrease its secretions, and this decrease—in girls at age 10 or

11, and in boys at age 12 or later—effects a chain of hormonal changes that last throughout adolescence. The changes come to an end when the growth hormone and testosterone in males decline at age 19, and when the growth hormone and estrogen decline at age 16 or 17 in females.

Notice the sequence of female hormonal events charted in the diagram below:

FEMALE HORMONAL CHANGES

1. Pineal gland decreases secretions at age 10 or 11.

2. Hypothalamus changes its secretions.

3. Pituitary gland releases trophic hormones.

4. Ovaries are stimulated to produce progesterone and estrogen.          Adrenals are stimulated to produce androgens.

There are several points to note about female development. First, puberty is achieved only after estrogen and other hormones are produced in major amounts. Second, adolescence begins early in females! The average age of beginning breast enlargement is 10.5 years. The first appearance in girls of a few pigmented hairs in the pubic region is 10.9 years. The average age of first menstruation (menarche) is 12.6 years, with 80 percent of girls achieving first menstruation between ages 11.0 and 14.0 years.

The beginning of menstruation is *NOT* related to the girl's stage of breast development, pubic hair development, or growth in height. Only rarely does a female have the ability to conceive at first menstruation, although this may occur. Normally there is an interval of puberal sterility of three years or more between first menstruation and first fertile ovulation. The growth hormone, estrogen, and other hormones are responsible for the growth spurt and development of sexual maturity in girls, but these hormones also play their part in their psychological development as well, by giving adolescent females extra energy. Varying amounts of testosterone, the so-called male sex hormone, are also produced in all females, but the amount is usually small.

Now notice the sequence of hormonal events *in males,* as charted in the diagram below:

MALE HORMONAL CHANGES

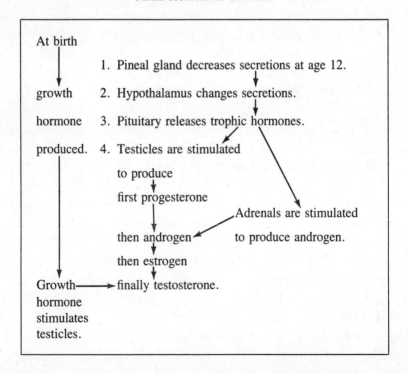

This diagram highlights several points that are important in understanding male adolescents. First, puberal change in males begins with an increase in the size of the testicles, and this increase commences shortly before age 12. Penis growth begins to increase in velocity at age 12.5 years and maximum penis size is attained at age 17.5 years. Sixty to 70 percent of all males experience breast enlargement around age 14, but this enlargement most always disappears by age 16. Pubic hair first appears in males at age 13.

Live sperm are evidenced in the urine in most males prior to the first ejaculation of sperm at age 13.5, but these quantities are usually small until age 14.5. The growth hormone partly controls blood plasma levels of testosterone. There is a marked decrease in blood plasma testosterone in most males between ages 19 and 20, when the growth hormone declines. Testosterone and other hormones contribute to psychological development as well as growth in height and sexual development. For example, testosterone increases energy, self-confidence, courage, and aggressiveness.

The biological unfolding of adolescence is not something parents can prevent or delay. The growth and changes are inevitable, and should be anticipated with excitement and optimism and guided with wisdom. Remember that God is at the helm of adolescence, and there is not one single aspect of adolescence that prevents you from enjoying your adolescent most of the time—dark days excepted.

## There Will Be a Few Dark Days

Paul and Elizabeth love and enjoy their 15-year-old daughter Melissa on most days. But how much must parents tolerate? Isn't there a limit of parental endurance? These parents always aimed at being "modern" parents with a progressive, enlightened approach. So when Melissa's bedroom looked like a war disaster zone, with an empty clothes closet and all the clothes thrown on the floor, her parents shut the door and said tolerantly, "If you want dirty clothes washed, Melissa, put them in the laundry room on wash day."

Melissa ignored them and wore soiled, smelly clothes to school.

Then one day a single, extra-small straw broke the camel's back. Paul caught the family dog going into Melissa's bedroom, digging in Melissa's litter, and burying pork chop bones under her piles of clothes and junk. Paul went into her room and started digging too. He found enough food scraps and bones to supply a six-dog sled team. Something snapped inside his head (this being his impractical "enlightenment" about parenting teenagers!), and this is what he did: he gathered up, washed, and securely locked away all of Melissa's clothes except one pair of jeans, two T-shirts, several sets of underclothing and socks, and one warm sweater. This handful was given to Melissa to wear for the next six months, along with the clothes she had on that day. As items of her clothing wore out, they were replaced from the large supply in storage. At the end of this six-month "lean" period, Melissa was ready to cooperate with her parents about the proper care of her clothing and her room.

This example of adolescent action and parent reaction is not unusual. Every parent could tell three or four stories of his own. But we have missed the point if we start thinking of adolescence as a stage of continual, endless conflict with parents. Adolescence is not, except in rare exceptions, a stage of conflict; it is a stage of growth, learning, maturation, and laughter. Paul and Elizabeth enjoyed Melissa all through those years of her growing up except for a few dark days. The rest was exciting and enjoyable. Even the day after the lockup of her clothes, they enjoyed each other—except for one exhausting hour of confrontation.

Yes, we need to be prepared for some very tough decisions,

some unpleasant moments, even a month or two of worry toward the end of adolescence, but we can thank God heartily that the battles are brief and the peace is long. Be ready to hold the line on matters of values and conscience, but do not accept the doom-and-gloom view of the teen years, namely, that they are all "storm and stress."

Adolescence is *not* all "storm and stress," and you can enjoy your teenager. *Enjoy* and *adolescent* are two words that should go together, and the chapters ahead show you how and why.

If you want to enjoy your teenager, study and follow the formula that is the basic chapter outline of this book. Here it is:

> If you love and understand them,
> and teach them,
> and accept them,
> and confront them,
> and release them,
> you will enjoy your teenagers.

# PART TWO

# Understand Them

Jill's mother walks in the door, tired but contented. She puts down a bag of groceries and video films, and asks Jill, age 15, and David, age 12, to come out to the car and bring in the rest of the groceries. It's Friday, and Mom congratulates herself on getting through another exhausting week at work.

"It's David's turn to help bring stuff in," whines fully grown Jill. Jill will help with household work only if she can't get out of it, and usually nags brother David to do it for her if he is available. David says, "I'm not moving unless she helps too, Mom, because I just did the dishes and walked the dog while Jill sat on her behind!"

## Understanding Their State of Mind

Mom listens. She is wise enough to have expected all of this, and she is ready with a good solution. Realistic expectations are part of good parenting, and Mom's expectations are realistic. She does not let her deep love for her children blind her to their real state of mind, their priorities, their reasoning, their blindness, and their illusions.

"Let's forget the stuff in the car for now. I need to sit down and put my feet up with a cup of tea and one of those oranges. Did Dad phone? Did the oven turn itself on in time, and how is that casserole cooking?'' After fifteen minutes Mom is rejuvenated, and she goes out to the car with Jill and David, who have been told that there will only be Friday night video films to watch when groceries are brought in and put away, when the table is set, *and* when the kitchen is cleaned up after supper. No arguments, no hassles, and no yelling—just Mom's firm statement of facts—and the near-crisis passes without insults, without injuries, and without losers. Jill knows threats don't work on Mom—she has already tried every kind of threat and blackmail without success. Tantrums don't work either—Mom ignores them. Stubbornness doesn't work—Mom is more stubborn, and if Jill were stubborn about the groceries in the car, Mom would just drive to the video store and return the videos immediately. Boy, were Jill and David surprised when she did just that last Christmas! Give Mom credit—she really understands how Jill and David think and feel. So there are no big blowups at home on this particular Friday night.

Nor is the evening spoiled by a steady stream of low-level insults, snide remarks, unfair demands, and false accusations. Jill, who is a master of innuendo, sarcasm, and pettiness, knows that Mom will call her bluff if she stoops to any of these verbal manipulations. Consequently, because of Mother's understanding of her two teens—her awareness, her perception, her firmness— none of these "pressure plays" spoil the family evening together. How well do you understand your teenagers? The chances are, if you understand them, you enjoy them—most of the time.

## Understanding Assumes That You Love Them

George, now 17½, has a good record of responsibility, and his parents are proud of him. Shortly after his sixteenth birthday, his parents told him that they were pleased with his behavior and wanted to try giving him *full* responsibility for managing his life. Did he think he was ready for such big responsibility? During the next eighteen months, George did manage his own life while still living at home. He came and went, chose his own friends and activities, and his parents are very pleased with the results in all but one area—MONEY.

George gets a fair amount of wages each Friday night for work he does, but he is always flat broke by Saturday. Yet Saturday night from seven to nine is George's favorite roller-skating time, and he is disappointed when Mom and Dad refuse to extend him any credit. George then tries the old "you don't love me" trick, half believing his own words as he tries vainly to separate a few dollars from his parents.

His father says to George, "If we say yes to you, it might mean we don't love you and we just want you off our back, but if we say no, then that definitely means that we love you. And no it is, George. You have the right to spend your funds as fast as you want. But when you are broke for whatever reason, it is simply not our responsibility. You must learn that money spent is money gone. Face the fact and guide yourself accordingly.

Afterward, Mom says privately to Dad, "Does he really question our love?" The truth of the matter is that sometimes teenagers *do* briefly question their parents' love, and when this occurs, parents can do no more than repeat the facts. "George, Mom and I love you more than we love anyone else in the world except each other, but love is not a shelter from truth and reality. We still have to tell you the truth, even if it causes you pain. We still must help you see reality, even if it's a weakness that is in yourself. Yes, we love you, but we know that love is never enough by itself. You need our understanding and wisdom too."

## If You Love Them, It Is Harder to Let Them Go

Mom is terrified to let her sixteen-year-old daughter have more freedom, and no wonder. Mom knows her daughter could easily ruin her future by fashioning unbreakable bad habits or by misfortunes such as a car accident. Mom knows of other parents who let go too soon and lived to regret it. But Mom also knows she has no choice. Either she lets go at a fair pace, or her daughter will break loose and walk out of the relationship. It is a dilemma: too fast is no good, and holding on too long is no good, and yet there is no set timetable to guide parents on how fast to let go. But Mom understands her daughter's desire for freedom, and Mom accepts that freedom as an inevitability. She prepares her daughter for the freedom, expands the freedom gradually, and confronts her daughter wisely when she slips and falls backward. The release from parental control actually takes place.

But a mother's love for her daughter has within it a real danger, in that love makes it harder for a parent to let a child go. The selfishness of love makes Mom want to keep her daughter for herself, while the unselfishness of love desires that her daughter be happy. The motivation of love causes Mom to think hard to try to save her daughter from pitfalls and pain. The energy of love makes Mom think hard to try to presolve all of her daughter's problems. Mom's love for her daughter actually makes it hard for Mom to let her daughter stand alone on her own two feet and take the consequences that go with freedom. Love tries to save the other person from pain, but Mom can overdo this. Daughter needs some pain too, and some discomfort, and some inconvenience, especially if these are resulting from her own freedom and choices. Mom learns, as she reviews their relationship, that her great love is no longer appropriate. It is now freedom's turn. When Mom forces herself to back off a little and give their relationship a comfortable distance, then it is her daughter's turn to struggle with her own responsibilities. The resulting pains and frustrations bring many of the illusions and excesses of adolescence to an end. Yes, teens do need us to love them through childhood, but in their adolescence they need us to show our love differently by letting them go. Don't let your great love for your teenage sons and daughters spare them their normal, necessary share of discomfort and frustration—or they may just stay in their adolescence for the next forty years.

# 2

## Teens Are on a Bridge

Are teenagers children or adults? The answer is: *neither.* They are their own developing persons, sandwiched in between childhood and adulthood. They are definitely not children, and they are definitely not mature adults. Parents make a grave error if they treat their teens like children, and it is just as serious a mistake to demand that they act like adults.

Cathy is as big as her mother, as smart as her mother, and is stronger physically than her mother, but Mother protects her and cares for her as if Cathy were age 4, not age 14. "Get up and get ready for school, dear . . . eat your breakfast . . . wear this . . . brush your teeth . . . don't forget your lunch . . . wear a jacket. . . ."

Cathy reacts, "My mother loves me, I know that, but does she have to breathe down my neck like this? Does she need to do my thinking for me? Does she believe I am brainless, that I have no sense of time or responsibility, no awareness of what it takes to look after myself? Does she honestly think I'm such a basket case that I can't even get myself ready for school in the morning?" Mother, after parenting for so many years, doesn't know when to quit. Mother thinks Cathy is still a child and Cathy's resentment grows.

We must understand teens if we are going to enjoy them, and understanding them means accepting the fact that they are no longer children. One diagrammatic view of adolescents uses overlapping circles.

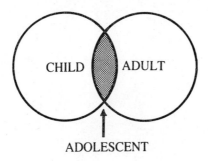

ADOLESCENT

This is NOT a useful way to view the teen years because adolescence is not merely an overlap. I believe that the series of circles below is a better picture of adolescence.

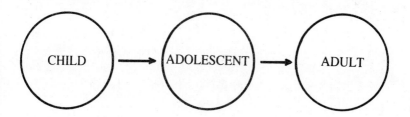

This series of circles is a better way to view adolescence, but the best picture of adolescence is the bridge analogy. The strength of the bridge analogy is that it suggests a time period, the time required to cross the bridge. If we portray the bridge as having many spans, we can picture the sub-stages of growing and maturing that characterize adolescence.

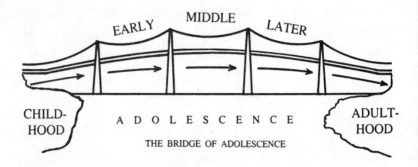

THE BRIDGE OF ADOLESCENCE

Adolescence means that we have stepped off the shore of childhood onto the bridge. We have left childhood behind, and we are on the move, traveling toward adulthood. The first span of the bridge is early adolescence, the next span is middle adolescence, and the final span is later adolescence. Adolescence is a lot of ground to cover, and it is a journey lasting a number of years.

## *Adolescere*—To Grow Into Maturity

The Latin word *adolescere* is a verb meaning to grow into maturity. Adolescence begins with sexual maturity and then proceeds to achieve, in rapid succession, physical maturity, intellectual maturity, self or identity maturity, and finally emotional maturity. In diagrammatic form, again using the analogy of the bridge, adolescence looks like this.

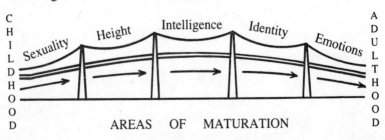

AREAS   OF   MATURATION

The timetable of maturity is very flexible and varies greatly from one adolescent to another. Persons are considered completely normal even when their own particular maturity is achieved two or three years *earlier* or four or five years *later* than the ages noted below.

---

MATURITY TIMETABLE FOR ADOLESCENCE

| | |
|---|---|
| Sexual Maturity | females: 11 to 14 years |
| | males: 13 to 15 years |
| Physical Maturity | |
|       Height | females: 14 years |
| | males: 16 years |
|       Girth or width | females: 17 years |
| | males: 19 years |
| Intellectual Maturity | females: 15 years |
| | males: 16 years |
| Self Identity Maturity | females: 17 years |
| | males: 20 years |
| Emotional Maturity | females: 19 to 23 years |
| | males: 20 to 25 years. |

---

Several points of explanation are required to understand this timetable. First, *intellectual maturity* refers to the achievement of maximum potential intelligence, which is achieved in the mid-teens. Intelligence includes learning, memory, and problem-solving ability, but does not include wisdom and good judgment, which normally reach their maximum in old age. Adolescents are intelligent but not usually wise. Teens can learn fast but adults "know" more, and adults usually have the practical experience that adolescents lack.

*Self* or *identity maturity* means that our character and personality have stabilized. We have settled, at least temporarily, on the roles, goals, and values we want to shape our future. We reserve the right to make changes, even major ones, but we have selected a self or character that we prefer, and we intend to use it as a base or reference point for further personal growth.

*Emotional maturity* is achieved as the limbic connectors in the brain develop fully in the early years of our twenties, interconnecting thinking, emotions, and memory in a pattern that makes for better self-control and self-understanding.

The process of achieving maturity in each of these five areas is a slow and gradual process that requires a number of years to complete. Maturity is not a sudden event or achievement; it is a slow process lasting a lifetime. What is unique about adolescence is the high speed of growth and maturity. Teens are maturing very quickly. As parents, we may be too close to them to appreciate what is happening.

## The Perpetual Adolescent

One major aspect of maturity—*thinking maturity*—deserves special consideration. Between ages 11 and 14, on the average, in both males and females, 50 percent of all adolescents experience a major growth and change in their thinking. Their thought processes are reorganized on a higher level of complicated but efficient logical thinking. After this change occurs, they are then able to reason in terms of possibilities, and they can sort through complicated problems and generate solutions. They understand the relationship between the real and the possible. They are able to weigh out the possible solutions they have created, and evaluate them according to general principles and abstract concepts. With their new thinking abilities they can apply general principles of ethics, of values, or of strategy to specific situations. This new adolescent thinking ability is the final stage of the development of thinking, and they will practice and perfect this type of thinking throughout their adult lives.

The other 50 percent of adolescents do not experience this major growth in thinking ability. They remain at the childhood level of thinking, which deals only in simplistic terms with the problems of life. They face problems by manipulating the situation by trial and error to see if there is a way to make the pieces fit together. "I'll try this way. No, it's not working. I'll try this other way. No, it's not working either. Well, maybe this way . . . there, it's working."

Those adolescents whose thinking does not mature pick an adult pattern of living that is full of routines and repetition and does not involve complicated choices. They choose this strategy because they have no ability to reason about principles in terms of possible consequences. Instead, their strategy is to operate without principles or merely to latch on to one principle if they notice that it appears to work for others.

Harvey, age 19, is a calm and reliable friend and employee who has hardly had a complicated thought in his life. He knows what he likes and dislikes, and moves forward in a straight line to what he likes. If his boss turns down one of Harvey's requests and offers Harvey reasons, Harvey is only interested in the bottom line: "Did I get it, or didn't I get it?" He is unable to expand to multi-perspective thinking. He only wants to know, "Either I got my request or I didn't. Which is it?"

Why is it that 50 percent of adolescents never reach the higher level of thought? Many adults who continue to think on a childhood level have vocabularies that are high in verbs and nouns. They prefer imperative forms of speech: "shut the door," "pass the milk," "don't touch that!" Their conversation is simple, direct, and obvious, and deals only with the concrete reality in front of them. Their thinking follows their speech pattern and is brief, direct, and devoid of complexities.

Those adults who have achieved the more complex levels of thinking have speech that is capable of clear distinctions in meaning because it makes full use of prepositions, adverbs, adjectives, conjunctions, and other forms of speech that refine and specify meaning. These adults use clauses and complex grammar and syntax to express themselves, and their thinking follows their speech in the ability to make careful definitions and specify exact shades and variations of meaning and intent.

Adult-level thinking seems to originate from the superior language skills used by some parents at home in the pre-school years. Those persons who learned to use all the parts of speech in early childhood with complexity and skill are the same ones who learn that higher level of thinking in adolescence. These superior language skills are rarely begun in later childhood but must be learned in early childhood.

We have, then, this important but unfortunate addition to the maturity timetable of adolescence: *Thinking maturity* occurs at age 12 to 14 years for roughly 50 percent of adolescents. The other 50 percent continue to think in the simplistic, direct, imperative style.

## The Bridge Has Many Spans

*Early adolescence* is the first span on the bridge, and in females covers the years 10 to 13, and in males covers the years 12 to 14. Puberty is achieved and the growth spurt is in full swing. A big leap forward in cognitive or thinking development takes place in 50 percent of adolescents. Early adolescents are grouping with same-sexed peers.

*Middle adolescence* covers the years 14 to 16 in females, and years 15 to 17 in males. The illusions and imbalances of adolescence are in full bloom, as these young people pursue their own identities and independence with determination. Groups of males are beginning to associate with groups of females in middle adolescence, and this paves the way for adolescent pairing in later adolescence. Middle adolescents need to be made responsible to work and make a major contribution to their own existence, or else they will overemphasize the social and sexual aspects of their lives.

*Later adolescence* begins for females in their seventeenth year and in males at age 18, and may last two to five years before adult maturity is reached, but early maturers often reach full maturity at age 18 or 19. Later adolescence is a time for adolescent pairing, falling in love a number of times, seeking to make decisions about career and marriage. Hormone levels drop dramatically, brain development is completed, and questions of identity are settled. Full maturity is around the corner.

There is, then, a three-spanned bridge of adolescence, or three distinct sub-stages within the adolescent period. Each of these stages has unique opportunities and typical problems for both adolescents and their parents. Let us now look carefully at the three sub-stages, allowing a full chapter for each of early and middle adolescence and two full chapters for later adolescence.

# 3

---

# The Search for Personal Identity

The very heart of early adolescence is the identity question, "Who am I?" Females at 11 to 13 and males at 13 to 15 are asking themselves questions about personal identity, uniqueness, and self-worth. Look at these questions of early adolescence:

1. Who am I?
2. Do I like who I am?
3. Who do I want to become?
4. Do I have the right to change my values, beliefs, attitudes, and habits?
5. What are my rights?
6. Will I leave home at 18?
7. Must I obey my parents?
8. I can think—at least—so what do I think about these questions?
9. My dad doesn't wear earrings, and my mom doesn't wear blue jeans. Should I dress and talk and act like my parents and their generation?
10. Should I dress, talk, and act like my friends at school?
11. Am I part of a new generation?
12. Can I be different from my parents while still living under their roof?
13. How much different can I become?

Gordon and Jill are parents who listen to their 12-year-old daughter Amy, and when they listen to her, they hear Amy's mind going over all these questions. Jill tends to be a worrier and Gordon is the calmer of the two; together they make a good parenting team. They keep themselves ready to listen to Amy, and if they are asked, they share their views with her. These parents know that the parent-child relationship is over. Why? Because Amy is no longer a child; she is an adolescent. So they help Amy to feel free, within limits, to explore carefully with them all the changing, growing, thinking, and questioning, and this is all as it should be. Amy will find the answers she is looking for, but the search will take years. She is seeking her own identity, and after much concern, doubt, frustration, laughter, and tears, she will find and create that identity. She will then spend the rest of her life strengthening, refining, and revising it.

In this second of seven chapters on understanding adolescents, we look at identity and adolescent idealism, which is their search for their own best self. Half of all early adolescents are becoming possibility thinkers, and their minds are searching all possibilities for the best possible life—best friends, best education, best job, best girlfriend, best car, most freedom. They do not want second best. They do not want to settle for anything less than the most they can possibly obtain and achieve within their own priorities and values. Their search for identity is an attempt to find a life-style, character, and values that they believe will maximize their own future happiness. Fortunately for them, they do not know all the tears ahead—tears and frustration that will result from the wrong decisions that they were so sure would take them in the best directions.

Adolescence is a time of hope and enthusiasm, because decisions are being made almost daily that have great promise for future fulfillment. But not enough time has elapsed for the adolescent to know whether the decision was a good one or one that was sure to result in regret. This "natural high" of adolescence—the excitement and dreamy-eyed exuberance, the abounding confidence of coming successes—has yet to be tested by the ultimate question: "Do the consequences of my decisions prove that my decisions were the right ones?" Only as time passes can any of us get confirmation of the rightness of our decisions, and adolescents are no different. They must wait and see if they are proved right as the consequences of their decisions unfold.

The abounding confidence of the teen years is finally replaced by a more cautious optimism (and periods of downright discouragement!) as errors in decision-making come back to painfully haunt us. The inexperience of adolescence usually results in many errors of judgment, and the frustration and discomfort of these errors bring the illusions of adolescence to an end. Hard reality ushers in adulthood. Parents would like to spare their children these discomforts, but this is not always possible. Some lessons must be learned the hard way, namely, by personal experience.

## I Know Who I Am Not

Sandra, age 13, says, "My mother seems to need me to be like her in every way. She pushes me to have her values, her ideas. But I am not my mother. I don't know who I am yet, but I know I am not my mother. I find myself getting very upset and put off when she is upset that we are different. She is like a detective who is searching for signs and evidence, and every time she finds another way that I am different, the fight is on."

Tony, age 15, is supersensitive about family pressure to conform, and he rebels against this conformity. It is not that he wants to rebel, but he does want to be unconventional as a way of giving himself space to become his own person. Tony says, "My dad and my older brother are carbon copies of each other. My brother is comfortable as he follows in Dad's footsteps, but

I am not. Perhaps in five years I will become another family clone, but now I need to experiment with ideas, styles, attitudes, trying one new thing and setting it aside, trying something else and setting it aside, until I find what really fits me as a person. I do not want to be like my brother and my parents.''

Most parents notice a resistance and negative reaction in their early teens, even if the parents are trying to do no more than keep some law and order in the family. This supersensitivity or reverse identification of adolescents is a natural, wholesome growth process which often causes gray hair and tears in parents, but is necessary in the discovery and development of the teenager's self.

It is as though the adolescent is saying, "Listen, Mom and Dad, I have been so dominated by your values and your attitudes in the past that I do not know how much of me is my childhood self, and how much of me is the person I want to become. So for a while I must take time to double-check all my basic assumptions, question everything, resist everything, until I decide what parts of me I will accept and what I will reject.''

As we noted earlier, this adolescent resistance is the exact opposite of childhood identification, and parents who remember how easy it was to parent their preadolescents wish they could turn back the clock. But never again!

Let us compare briefly the child and adolescent attitudes to those of parents. First, how do children develop their identity? Not by direct instruction and training by parents! Rather, they develop their identity by reaching out in naive acceptance and taking into themselves those essential aspects of the personalities around them. They internalize their parents' values, attitudes, beliefs, and habits by an imitative learning process known as identification. Look at those three words, *internalize, imitate,* and *identify.* Together these words describe the primary process of social learning in children which we call identification. In its very simplest form, identification takes place when a loving child follows in his parents' footsteps, copies their behavior, and tries to be like them. Identification also takes place in *any* direction where there are models that the child desires to follow. Identification means children have an inherent openness or naive readiness to adopt as their own certain traits and characteristics of others.

But how do teenagers develop their identity? Not by identification as children do, but rather by thinking about it. Thinking is central to adolescent learning. They think, reason, analyze, evaluate, and compare. They may perform these functions poorly and illogically because of inexperience, but their goal is to think things through clearly and make decisions on the basis of their thinking. They do not want simply to accept, to believe, to trust, to copy, to imitate as they did in childhood. Now they want evidence, reasons, facts, sound arguments, before they will change their behavior and character. This new power of thinking by which early adolescents can reason about principles, concepts, beliefs, and values makes them determined to be thinkers and not merely followers who imitate and copy others.

Another ability of adolescents plays an important role in the development of their identity. Not only can they think, which is fundamentally new for them, but they can think about what others are thinking. They can think about the thoughts of their parents, provided that their parents have spoken up and expressed their views. After a discussion, teens can walk away and consider the logic and evidence of the parents' point of view. So adolescents no longer learn by identifying with parents, but they can still learn from parents by hearing what the parents say and deciding for themselves if the argument merits acceptance.

In an oversimplified way we can here state, while acknowledging the danger of oversimplification, that children need parents to be good role models and good examples, the kinds of examples that cause the children to identify with parents.

Teenagers also need good role models, but they need at least one thing more, namely, they need their parents to be good talkers, who can explain their point of view in language that adolescents can understand and that persuades the teenagers of the soundness of their argument. Adolescents need their parents to speak out in favor of parental values, beliefs, attitudes, and habits. Parents should not give up trying and therefore leave their teens at the mercy of peers and the mass media. But it is only the strength of the parents' arguments that will persuade, not the fact that they as parents are making these points. And parents must try harder than peers or the mass media, because adolescents have a natural, necessary resistance to believing something just because parents say it is so. "We're not #1, so we try harder," said Avis Rent-a-Car. Parents are in the same situation, so they too must try harder.

Do not take your teen's resistance personally. Their purpose is not to hurt you, but to find themselves. They do not love you less, they love you differently. Let them begin to think, to think for themselves. Let them think, but *be sure to tell them what you think*. They are not mind readers. They need you to say what you think, and they need you to argue for what you believe.

## I Must Become My Own Person

The search for personal identity is not just an adolescent search. Every one of us at any age is working at finding, developing, and improving his inner self. Then why is special attention given to adolescents as they search for their identity? The reason is that teenagers must suddenly be extra sure of who they are and what they want because of puberty and sexual maturity. The life-shaping decisions that surround sexual activity, pregnancy, commitment, and marriage are rapidly approaching, and the great adolescent identity search is God's way to prepare adolescents for wiser decision-making in the years ahead.

Adolescents are already experiencing both internal and external sexual pressures, and they must be stronger in order to handle these pressures wisely. When sexual pressures intensify, then teenagers must decide about sex not on the basis of what others want for them, but in terms of what they themselves believe is best. Adolescent resistance, to parents especially, is simply good practice and experience in the whole art of resisting. This practice of resisting builds and strengthens the skills of resisting, and increases the likelihood that teens can say no. This word *no* is first learned at age 2, and it is the great word of lasting happiness. The ability to say no to self and to others is part of a good foundation upon which to build a future.

Adolescents, as they search for identity, uniqueness, and self-worth, must get stronger in the skill of making their own decisions. The multitude of disagreements with parents has the good result of teaching adolescents to think, listen, think some more, listen some more, and then make their own decisions, regardless of the intense pressure from the other person. Every parent wants his teenager to have the moral character and fortitude to say no, but the frustrating thing is that the adolescents must first learn to say no to parents!

"The nerve of that pipsqueak to say no to me," says Terry when his 15-year-old is resisting Terry's infallible wisdom. In later years, however, Terry is a happy parent as he sees that same son becoming his own person, able to make his own decisions, able to resist temptation, able to take a strong stand and say no in a high-pressure situation. "I must become my own person," says the son, and that has to start at home!

## We Create Our Own Character

The heart of identity is character, and character is a choice. Rather, character is the result of countless choices of childhood, adolescence, and adulthood. Each of us creates his own character; we are not born with it. Neither is our character given to us by parents, heredity, or environment. We make choices, and we become the kind of person we want to be.

The great adolescent search for a personal identity is part of the lifelong process of finding, developing, and improving our character. Children, adolescents, adults—all of us are engaged in the identity search for a strong and workable character.

What is character, and how does character develop? Character is the cluster of at least four basic parts of self:

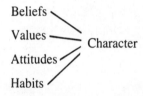

Adolescents have been developing these four parts of character since infancy, but in adolescence, character is deepened, broadened, refined, and enriched. Character begins in infancy. We create our first version of our character in infancy (birth to 14 months) and toddlerhood (14 months to 30 months), and then we change, revise, and strengthen our character in every subsequent stage of life, even into old age.

Character begins and develops as we make choices—consciously and unconsciously—about the kind of person to become. Early childhood is important in character development because it is the beginning of character. The small child observes the important people in his life and borrows whole chunks of their character—borrowing one aspect of character from one parent, other aspects of character from the other parent, still other "characteristics" from brothers, sisters, grandparents, baby-sitters, and others. The small child's efforts to build character by borrowing from the character of others are tentative efforts, not final. The child "tries on" traits of character like items of clothing, and may then accept, and later reject, these traits.

By age 2 usually, and almost always by age 3, most children have settled on an initial character for themselves. This beginning, baseline character that they have chosen for themselves is their first, basic, personal identity. Further character changes use this basic personal identity as a reference point from which to make all future changes.

Early adolescents have a major crisis of character because their physical growth, sexual maturity, and greater intelligence are all pushing them to have a much stronger character. The parents' proper task during the adolescent identity crisis, which is the subject of the last five chapters of this book, is to react and respond honestly—at times *accepting* adolescent changes, at times *confronting,* but always *understanding* the necessity of their search for their own identity.

All of life, not just early adolescence, is a challenge to continual improvement to the soundness, depth, consistency, and workability of our character. Adults throughout their life span are working on their characters too. The key word is *change,* especially *character change.* We create our own character, and we can also change that character. What an exciting challenge life is: the choices are ours and we struggle to become the best person possible! It is never too late to change and grow. New life is always possible for those who will consider change.

Your character represents your choice of the kind of person you want to be. This point is important, because it means each of us is fully responsible for his character. Character is a choice; therefore, you are responsible for your character.

Do you understand your teenagers? Do you understand that adolescence is a special time for them to evaluate their own character by means of their new thinking ability? One-half of all adolescents have new powers of thinking, and they soon turn these powers toward self-evaluation and possible change.

The other teens are not trying to change as much as they are trying to gain acceptance of their need for independence, so they can pursue freely what they want without interference from parents. This 50 percent of adolescents are not concerned primarily about possible self-growth and change; they only want to enjoy the present and increase their opportunities. Parents can help this group, not by prodding them toward inner change, but by helping them to understand and accept community and social requirements for employment, money management, and all "outward" aspects of life management.

# 4

# Breaking the Ties of Emotional Dependence

The growth and development of adolescence is always in the same direction and in the same sequence: first, identity growth in early adolescence; then growth of emotional freedom in middle adolescence; and finally, growth in the capacity and need for intimacy in later adolescence. In diagrammatic form, the phases are described as follows:

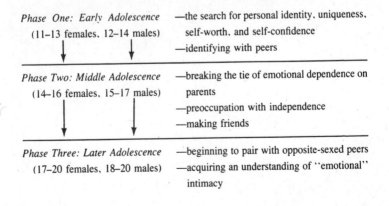

*Phase One: Early Adolescence*
(11–13 females, 12–14 males)

—the search for personal identity, uniqueness, self-worth, and self-confidence
—identifying with peers

*Phase Two: Middle Adolescence*
(14–16 females, 15–17 males)

—breaking the tie of emotional dependence on parents
—preoccupation with independence
—making friends

*Phase Three: Later Adolescence*
(17–20 females, 18–20 males)

—beginning to pair with opposite-sexed peers
—acquiring an understanding of ''emotional'' intimacy

## First Identity, Then Freedom

Middle adolescence has its own focus—the search for emotional freedom from parents. This focus on freedom is a natural consequence of success in the earlier search for identity. Meet Claire, age 14, who has succeeded in her search for identity and is just now beginning to focus and act like a middle adolescent, pity her parents! She values privacy and seeks to exclude parents from major areas of her life. She wants to make her own decisions, even if she is wrong. She resents her parents' fears for her safety, her health, her reputation, and her future. She is trying to prove to herself that she can survive without her parents' approval, and she wants to break the tie of emotional dependence on them.

Her need now, as Haim Ginott used to say, is *not to need her parents.* This is not a need for financial freedom, because she knows and accepts that she needs financial help (with strings attached that include chores and other ways of helping her family). It is not a need for political freedom, because she knows and accepts the fact that parental control in certain areas of her life will continue for a few more years yet. It is a need for *emotional freedom,* and is a psychological battle that Claire must fight within herself.

However, being young and inexperienced, she does not know that her battle is within herself, so she is one day battling her parents as though they were the problem, and the next day is battling siblings, and the day after, battling peers. Her days are frequently turbulent and full of interpersonal chaos, and to an untrained observer, it might not appear as though Claire is making progress, but she is. With each passing day, she loves her mother just as much but needs her mother's love a little less. With each passing day, she enjoys her mother's approval but needs this approval less and less. She is steadily becoming less responsive to her mother's emotional responses and emotional demands, and emotional freedom is then just around the corner for her.

## What Is Emotional Freedom?

Claire probably has no idea that the changes in her emotional relationship with her parents are part of God's perfect plan for her growth and maturity, but here she is, programmed by many internal time clocks of genetics and biochemistry, fighting her battle for emotional freedom right on schedule. Her parents do understand, it is hoped, that their daughter's need for emotional freedom is part of God's plan. Their better understanding helps them to know in what ways to let go and when. It also helps them to know in what ways *not* to let go and how to hang on to certain types of control a little longer.

What is emotional freedom, and how does it work best? Emotional freedom is the proper relationship of emotional independence between parents and their adolescent offspring. This emotional freedom becomes much stronger in middle adolescence and then expands significantly into full emotional freedom in later adolescence.

Full emotional freedom means that only mutual love and mutual respect remain as ongoing emotional ties of family. Emotional dependency is gone forever, except for a few emergencies and unforeseen contingencies of the future, such as accidents or crippling disease. In fact, dependency may even be reversed, as parents in their closing years begin to depend on offspring.

Emotional freedom means that the person no longer depends upon parents for love, concern, and approval. Loss of parental love and approval is no longer a critical concern, and the parents' remaining control over adolescents becomes more and more financial and political. In all likelihood, the parents' withdrawal of *political support* (such as, "You cannot continue to live in this house unless you stop such and such behavior") or *financial support* (such as, "If you want this kind of financial assistance from us, you must behave this way") would be a greater pressure than the withdrawal of *emotional support.*

The parents' refusal to cooperate with the gradual appropriate increase in emotional freedom is a serious error. They must work toward emotional freedom based on their assessment of the uniqueness and differences of each of their children. But moving too slowly (or too quickly) in granting emotional freedom will have predictable, negative results.

Doug, age 13, is a good example of a child whose parents moved too quickly in granting emotional freedom. Doug's parents' great love for him, when added to their passive, pliable nature, misled them down the road to excessive generosity in parenting. Then, with a touch of martyrdom and shortsightedness, they made too few demands upon Doug, and lowered their expectations of him whenever he kicked up a fuss.

By age 13, Doug was in charge of his family, and his parents could not oppose him. He walked with a swagger, abused parents and friends, and reeked of arrogance, smugness, and superiority. Fortunately, the school system in their small town had a counseling and guidance staff who saw the collision course Doug was pursuing, and wisely intervened. Doug and his family then received counseling that bolstered the parents' self-confidence and assertiveness and subdued Doug just enough that he could balance his normal, healthy concerns about self with a counter-balance of concern for his parents and others.

Communities have many children like Doug, who strive for emotional freedom months and years before they are able to handle it. The whole problem is so complicated that parents *do* need to ponder and agonize over how quickly they should allow their teens the privacy and emotional distance they need to be separate persons and stand alone. The answers are never easy, and the fears of parents are realistic: freedom that comes too soon can ruin a life. Bad habits learned in youth can be forged of chains so strong that they cannot be broken in later years without supreme effort.

Of equal concern are those families who cling to one another too long. Emotional dependency is like a disease to such families, because the parents hang on too long and the adolescents do not break away. Such adolescents are in just as serious a situation as the aggressive Dougs of the world, but the passive adolescents are unnoticed because of their quietness, obedience, and conformity.

## Freedom Is a Bore, Unless You Haven't Got It

Only slaves are preoccupied with freedom; those who are free think not of freedom but of the opportunities and responsibilities that go with it. Adolescents desire to leave behind them the controlling limitations of childhood, and all they can think of now is:

- Paddle your own canoe.
- Take charge of your life.
- Be a woman; be a man.
- Don't hang on to mother's apron strings.
- Cut the umbilical cord.
- Decide your own destiny.
- *Tuum Est*—It is entirely up to you.

Their focus is emotional independence from parents. They want to be free so that later they can give their love to someone else. They want to shift their focus from parents to peers, from an older generation to their own generation. And there is not enough room for both generations to share first place.

Middle adolescence is the only phase of life when persons desire to be emotionally unattached and stand alone. But as soon as the emotional detachment from parents is accomplished and freedom is a fact, freedom becomes a bore, and the search begins for that special someone who will end emotional independence and revive emotional dependence.

Middle adolescence is nearing an end when emotional independence is achieved. But every person soon discovers that freedom and aloneness do not bring happiness. Independence does not bring happiness, and that is why independence must be only a brief stopover on the road back to mutual dependence. The goal of middle adolescence—emotional freedom—is a short-term goal only. Having broken the emotional dependence on parents, teens soon move on to search for a partner with whom they may be emotionally interdependent. The real goal of life is not independence but satisfying mutual dependence. But before they can achieve a mutual dependence with an opposite-sexed peer, the tie of emotional dependence upon parents must be broken.

## Yes, Mom, You Are Being Rejected

Many parents feel heartbroken when they see that their teen-agers are changing their focus of interest and attention away from the family. Parents wonder if this change of focus is a form of rejection. Of course it is, but not in any absolute sense, and it does have a bright side.

   Adolescents are on the right track and are moving in a natural, healthy, wholesome direction when they move their parents out of the number one position of interest and attention. The former intensity of the parent-child relationship is no longer appropriate for adolescence and adulthood. Parents must slowly fade into a lesser significance, and every parent who notices this fading process under way should heave a huge sigh of relief because it is living proof that God's time clocks of normal development are keeping good time.

   The breaking of the tie of emotional dependency is essential for life to move forward: it is a positive, not a negative. First, the diapers were put away, then the small child learned to go out to play, then he went to school, now he breaks the dependency tie. Later he will move away from home.

   All of parenting, from infancy to adolescence, is a step-by-step preparation toward independent living. This can be the parents' finest hour, if, wanting to hold them close, we let them go; if, wanting them at our side, we encourage a comfortable distance; if, wanting to be involved in all of their busy doings, we allow them privacy. Yes, Mom, you are being rejected, but afterward they will still love you as much as ever. But you will never again be in first place, and your encouragement and support will be important on fewer and fewer future occasions. So take it on the chin: it will hurt to break the habit of parenting. But this is an important time to keep close check on yourself:


- Don't love them too much.
- Don't hold them too close.
- Keep them at a comfortable distance.
- Allow them privacy.
- Accept your lesser role, and let them know you approve of the

new type of parent-teen relationship. Loosen your grip, let them go, and be proud of yourself for doing so.

- Expect them to come back for hugs, counsel, comfort, or solace a few times as the usual crises of life hit them. In such cases hug them and love them, and again let go.

## Assist Your Teens Toward Freedom

Listen to Chad, age 17: "My parents stick to me like flypaper. They want me around to talk and discuss. I need them to become absorbed in doing their own thing, so I can feel free to consider all my options." Parents can assist their teens toward emotional freedom by setting their own lives in directions which do not include their teens.

Listen to Joanne, age 15: "I still love my mom as much as ever, but I want our relationship to take less time and energy. I want to enjoy her company in very small amounts, and I don't want her to cry when my life is moving away from her in new directions." Parents can encourage emotional freedom by accepting and approving the wider spacing and distancing their teens structure to separate them from their parents. Parents, learn to accept this distancing without comment. Your silence is acceptance enough.

Gail's parents assisted her toward emotional independence when she was 16 by reducing their expressions of concern when she was upset or confused. "Gail, we are pleased that you are getting so much wiser. We worry a little at times, yes, but our main feeling is confidence that you can exercise good judgment and self-control. You can handle most of these problems yourself; at this stage you only need Mom and me as a sounding board. Go ahead and make your decision, and then work out the details as you go along. You don't really need us to help you to decide, but we are here to listen.''

## Liberty Breeds Giants

Do you want your sons and daughters to find maximum emotional maturity? Then give them as much emotional freedom along the way as is practical and wise. Only liberty breeds giants, and only emotional freedom generates emotional maturity. Your offspring cannot enjoy maximum emotional maturity unless you give them as much head space and heart space as you dare, while making allowance for their age and present maturity.

"There is a right time for everything . . ." (Ecclesiastes 3:1 TLB), so take the risk, and wisely loosen your grip. Watch them carefully, and as they show that they understand and benefit from your move, then loosen more and finally let go. Sheltering, smothering, coddling, indulging, and overprotecting have no place in a plan for maximum emotional maturity.

Remember that the test of freedom is their right to make mistakes. You must not tighten your grip if they move in unwise directions and make mistakes. But you also have a right—the right to be available if they come temporarily back into your heart a few times when they are weak and unsure. Then, after they are reassured briefly, they will try again, and you must again let go.

# 5

# Awaiting
# Romantic Love

Sigmund Freud was once asked, "What should a normal person be able to do well?" He answered immediately in German: *"Lieben und arbeiten"* (To love and to work).

As Erik Erikson, the specialist in adolescent development, pondered Freud's answer, he decided that this is what Freud meant:

> *"He meant productiveness, balanced and integrated with the capacity to be a sexual and loving being."*

In this chapter on love and intimacy, and in the next chapter on meaningful work, we sharpen our understanding of *later adolescence*, the years from 17 to 18 for females, and the years 17 to 20 for males. These are the critical years for learning to love and learning to work. The Creator has programmed young minds in these years to pursue learning and skill in both of these areas.

## Adolescents Must Learn to Love

Some adolescents are more fortunate than others because they have already learned much about love and marriage from the good example of their parents' marriage. Others are less fortunate and have learned a sour view of love. To grow up with parents who dearly love each other and express their love in a wholesome way is the finest way to learn about love.

But even the most fortunate teens must learn by doing. They must begin to develop friendships with opposite-sexed peers, and some of these friendships will develop into loving relationships. The adolescent must have the opportunity to be with others his own age, because learning to love is both theory-learning and apprenticeship-training. There must be opportunities to fraternize, to socialize, to laugh, to tease, to discuss, to challenge, to persuade, to study, to change, to allure, to love. Later adolescence is the perfect time to pursue friendships and love with opposite-sexed peers. High school and church are good places for this process to begin because of the supervision and the large numbers of adolescents available.

What learning is necessary?

Later adolescents must learn *comfort and low anxiety* with opposite-sexed peers. As early adolescents, they had high anxiety and discomfort with opposite-sexed peers, and so they fraternized with friends of their own gender. But now is the time for older teens to learn to relax and be comfortable with opposite-sexed peers. This means learning to enjoy closeness. It means beginning to learn to make one other human being special and to favor that person over all others—a partner, a comrade, a lover, a person who is "number one," another human being who is so close that there is almost a fusion of two identities into one.

A whole cluster of interrelated social and interpersonal skills must be learned, practiced, and perfected:

1. learning to trust more deeply
2. learning to express emotions honestly

3. learning to communicate—to talk, to listen, to share, to understand
4. learning to cooperate and compromise
5. learning to confront constructively
6. learning to forgive and forget
7. learning to let the other person grow and change
8. learning to place commitment on a higher level than love
9. learning that sex never precedes total commitment, that is, marriage

This is only a partial list of relationship skills, but it is long enough to demonstrate that older teens must give attention to learning to love or they will not be able to develop skill in these important areas.

## Emotional Intimacy Now, Sexual Intimacy Later

The word *intimacy* used to mean an intense closeness of two persons, but now it tends to mean sexual activity. However, if we stick with the former meaning of intimacy, namely, intimacy as closeness, then it is a better word than love to describe the intertwining and interweaving of two minds. Adolescents need to practice this *mental intimacy*—an intimacy of thought and intimacy of emotions—which precedes and is a foundation for the love, commitment, and sex that comes in marriage. First should come mental or emotional intimacy, a meeting of minds which includes development of mutual understanding and appreciation, an exciting process where two separate minds reach out to each other and seek to know, understand, and enjoy each other. It is a beautiful, hesitant process that is eager but unsure, excited but in control, a process that seeks to know the other person and be known as well. *Emotional intimacy*—the meeting of minds, the matching of minds, the testing of minds—is the only adequate foundation for marriage. That is why the practice of emotional intimacy must be a priority in later adolescence.

Why should sexual intimacy wait for marriage? This is an important question for this generation because of the changing sexual standards of society. The biblical Christian view of sex is: first, a meeting of minds, including mutual understanding, leading to love; then, commitment, leading to marriage; then, sex.

Psychological and biological research confirm the wisdom of the biblical, Christian view. However, it is not enough to answer the question, "Why should sexual intimacy come later?" by saying, "The Bible says so." The Bible does say so, that is true, but the question is, "Why?"

Here are some reasons why sexual intimacy should come within marriage:

1. Sexual intimacy interferes with the development of emotional intimacy. Minds should explore each other first, but this important, elaborate process of getting to know each other virtually grinds to a halt as soon as sexual intimacy begins. When two persons are still strangers, they first need to get to know each other's minds, including values, beliefs, attitudes, and habits, so they can wisely decide if they might form a successful partnership.

People who have sex from the beginning of their relationship often don't "know" each other except in the sexual sense; their minds are still many miles apart. No wonder common-law marriages often flounder after a legal wedding: they never attained that meeting of minds upon which to build a life together. Some think a marriage certificate will miraculously change the other person, but it never happens that way.

2. Sexual activity, when it occurs early in relationships, interferes with "falling in love." It is sexual tension, especially in males, that motivates us to pursue the mental intimacy and meeting of minds that is the basis of love. Note: *sexual tension*, not sexual satisfaction, *leads to love,* and early sex is often the

proverbial kiss of death to the deepening of the relationship.

Leanne found this out the hard way when she had sex with Mark on their third date. She said to herself, "I just know Mark will love me if I go to bed with him and have his baby." From then on, Leanne was horrified to discover that Mark had only sex in mind when they went out together, and Leanne understood that there was now no way they could build the relationship further.

How does sexual satisfaction interfere with "falling in love"? We fall in love mainly because we *admire the mind,* not the body, of that special person. Admiration is the basis of love, and love grows when there is a meeting of minds resulting in *mutual admiration.* Admiration reflects our sense of values; it is our evaluation of the worth of another person, and high admiration added to emotional intimacy begins a heart attachment of love.

It is important to see that the heart attachment starts in the head, not in the genitals. The mind—with appraisal, imagination, fantasy, and memory—begins an attachment to the other mind based on admiration. Out of this mental attachment should come the total commitment that paves the way for sex. Emotional intimacy first, then the total commitment of marriage, then sex. And what is the most satisfying sex of all? That which occurs between two persons who are deeply in love and totally committed.

*Admiration and sexual tension* are the chief ingredients of falling in love. Then comes commitment in marriage, and then comes sex. This is the proper sequence, from a biblical Christian point of view, and from the psychological and biological points of view as well.

## Parents May Be Afraid

Parents have every reason to be afraid when their later adolescents begin the serious work of learning to relate closely to opposite-sexed peers. But this is no time to panic or to try to hang on to them tightly. Adolescents do eventually learn the skills of emotional intimacy; they learn by listening, by experimentation, by trial and error. They learn some skills easily, and they learn other skills only by tears and heartache.

The greatest blessings of natural life—marriage, family, and parenting—are worth all of the risk of being hurt, the danger of learning wrong habits, and the frustration of being rejected and misunderstood. Parents, back off and let your children learn. Do not hurry them or slow them down too much. Do not crowd them, rather give them space. On the days of their sorrows be available to listen, but be slow to give advice. Let them know you have confidence in them to be able to bear the pain without bitterness.

# 6

## The Need for Meaningful Work

What do adolescents want? They want to make a significant contribution. They want to do something that will prove they can contribute to their own life and their community. They want to do meaningful, challenging work.

Then why does Mark, age 13, balk at cleaning his bedroom and taking out the garbage? Because he thinks that these two activities prove he cannot contribute anything of *real* value, and he is ashamed and embarrassed to do this simple, unskilled, insignificant work.

For many years of his childhood, Mark watched his parents monopolize the significant household work, and he was given the trivial, unimportant things to do. He could sweep the floor but he couldn't cook because he might burn the cookies and therefore waste food. He could clean the basement or pick up the dog feces in the backyard, but he couldn't do the laundry because he might use too much soap, or he might wash woolens and shrink them.

Over the years, his parents gave him the message that he was incapable of doing many household tasks. He was only allowed to do tasks so simple that no skill was required, or so insignificant that even if they were done poorly, it didn't matter.

Adolescents have a natural eagerness to do adult work, important work, work that makes a valuable contribution to family life. Many parents cultivate and nurture this natural eagerness, and other parents stamp it out. Darren, age 14, is already operating his father's hay baler. Darren begged and begged for the chance to do this important, dangerous work, and so both parents hesitantly agreed that he could do so. After all, he had sat for countless hours in the tractor cab with Dad as they went hay-baling together.

So his parents taught him and coached him on many safety points, and Darren went and baled hay. Yes, he had a few more breakdowns than Dad would have had. Yes, he had to have Dad's help at times. Yes, the big round bales looked a little lopsided. But what was the state of Darren's mind? Darren was incredibly happy to do this important work.

Many years later when Darren was operating his own farm, he realized that the reason he loved farming was because he had always been allowed to do the significant work, and was praised and given recognition for what he did. How does this compare with his friends on the next farm, who finally graduated to weeding and hoeing the small vegetable garden and fetching the cows? No wonder his friends hated farming. No wonder his friends hated work.

## Presidents Don't Take Out the Garbage

Why are adolescents so touchy, so sensitive about the kinds of work they are willing to do? They are touchy because they are so insecure. This worn-out word *insecure* seems so contradictory when applied to teenagers. George, age 17, "knows" at least a hundred times as much as his father on any subject. George even knows more about subjects he has never heard of before!

It sounds preposterous to think of George as insecure when he is always calling himself the genius. "I'm a genius, Dad, I am definitely a genius," he says with a nervous laugh, but behind all the bravado, the big showy exterior of confidence, is a young man who isn't sure if he can pass the critical test: can he acquire competence in a work role that will earn him a living in the competitive world of employment?

George doesn't want to take out the garbage or do any menial, simple, minor tasks. He does want to wash the car, and change the oil and filter. He does want to do the grocery shopping. He will get a full supper ready for the family, but hates to do the dishes afterward. He knows what he wants, and may not be too mature in some of his wants, but he is on the right track in looking for things to do in the family that are essential, important, significant tasks. In his insecurity, he thinks of his personal worth as an extension of the kind of work he does: "Presidents don't take out the garbage."

George's real satisfaction comes on Saturday mornings if his father takes him to the family business, a small welding shop where Father rebuilds diesel engine heads. George is content to clean up the shop, but beams with pride if he can do some welding, drive the tow truck, or just talk to customers. In doing these tasks, George is confident that he is moving in the right direction. "After all," thinks George to himself, "if I'm doing the same work that Dad does to earn us all a living, then that must prove that I'm going to make it in the world of work."

## Work Must Be Meaningful

North American society does not believe in the importance of work in the adolescent stage, and so the only meaningful work provided for teens by this society is schoolwork and book learning. Is schoolwork truly acceptable work for adolescents? Of course it is. Schoolwork is preparatory to the real work that comes later, and schoolwork is legitimate work which anticipates a meaningful contribution in the future.

Teens and families are wise to believe in hard work at school. But what about the 50 percent of all adolescents who are not intellectually equipped to pursue academic studies? School is a tragedy and a waste of time for many of them, because they lack the complex skills of possibility-thinking that lead to success in academic pursuits. These teenagers do not learn by reading, thinking, and discussing; they learn by doing. Meaningful work for this half of adolescents is either *apprenticeship training or actual manual labor for wages.* How terrible these doer-adolescents feel about themselves if they accept society's error and believe that schoolwork is the only way to learn. These doers are beautiful in their own way, and they have every bit as much potential for a meaningful contribution to society as the reader-talkers. But society favors the reader-talkers.

Another legitimate form of work for adolescents is *sports.* Richard, age 16½, takes his highly organized Tier One Junior League Hockey as extremely serious work. Maureen, age 15, works at her gymnastic skills and her team contribution, and it is all serious business for her. Chris, age 15, plays intramural basketball, which is mainly for fun, sportsmanship, and fellow-ship, and Chris has no aspirations to be another Magic Johnson. But even though they won't become pros, the intramural players get to all their practices, and they give their best effort to support their team and their coach. Each of these young people is gaining from athletics a sense of accomplishment and an opportunity to practice many interpersonal living skills that will relate directly to their success in their future work.

*Volunteer work* is another excellent sphere for adolescent endeavor, and includes Christian volunteer work of all types, health-related work with the young, the handicapped, the de-prived, the needy, and the aged.

*Music and the arts* are also excellent areas for teen involvement, providing a sense of accomplishment by perfecting skills and performing for the enjoyment of others.

Finally, every teenager should be pushed, nudged, cajoled, persuaded, and rewarded to *contribute to the work of his own household*. Adolescents should make a major contribution whenever this is possible. Each of them is capable of learning all the skills of homemaking, so parents should teach and supervise teens until they are proficient in all areas of helping around the home. True, it is more work for parents to teach and supervise adolescents than just to go and do the work themselves. But the point is that teenagers have to be taught at home, and parents are the only ones to teach them about homemaking.

Are you getting your teen to work at home? If your adolescent appears to be lazy with a bad case of TV-itis, what could you do differently to help him or her get a positive attitude toward work?

## Work Improves Attitudes

No wonder Carla, age 16, is so down on herself, lacking in self-confidence, and resentful of others. She is wasting her youth in trivial pastimes and she knows it. Her parents make life easy for her because their own life was so tough, "and we don't want her to have it as tough as we did." She is careless, bored, often arrogant, frequently hostile, and most of all, she feels utterly useless. This feeling of uselessness is based on reality, because Carla is in fact useless to herself and everyone else. She contributes nothing at home except complaints, excuses, and lies. She makes C's in her high school courses on one half hour of effort per day! She considers herself "not the type" to give her best effort in sports or volunteer work. She is useless.

Compare Carla with Cindy, who is only five months younger. Look at Cindy's busy life:

- Every day: make supper, do homework
- Saturday: help clean house
- Various days: teach swimming to the handicapped three times
    a week
        once a week, school band, piano lessons, cre-
            ative writing club, and archery club
        church, Wednesday, and Sunday
        boyfriend, at school and Friday evening

Cindy's attitude toward self is modest but positive. She is pleased to be who she is and to pursue her life as she is building it. She finds satisfaction in her activities, and this leads her to believe that she is acquiring competence in many of the skills essential to a full life. She knows she has good reason to be proud of herself because she is paddling her own canoe, paying her way by giving of herself in many real and significant ways. She has discovered that good work improves attitudes, and work keeps her on an even keel in her attitude toward self and others.

## Work Should Counterbalance Love

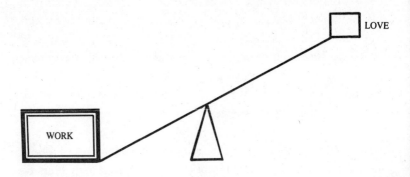

Look at this imbalance of work and love. It reminds us of Jack: "All work and no play makes Jack a dull boy." Adolescence should not resemble drudgery of a slave-labor camp. There must be time for leisure and love.

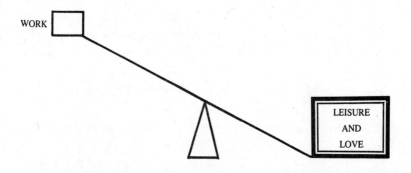

This imbalance reminds us of many of today's adolescents, who are denied the opportunity to find meaningful, satisfying work. If work is not possible, every teen will be preoccupied with sex and love even more than is normal for this stage.

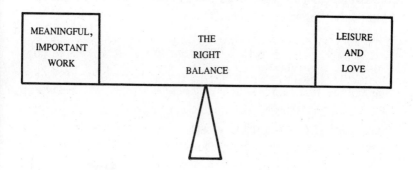

Later adolescence (age 17 to age 18 for females, and age 17 to age 20 for males) must have a dual emphasis on work *and* love. Later adolescence is the time for teens to get into the full swing of work, including working for a living, working and helping in the family, serving Christ through a New Testament congregation, and all other honorable forms of work.

When meaningful work is possible for adolescents, work counterbalances love. Does love need to be counterbalanced? Yes! New love needs to be slowed down. Young love needs to be cooled off. The young mind needs to be filled with counterbalancing thoughts so that love is built up slowly, carefully, and wisely. Young bodies and young minds need hard work, and then they need to rest and sleep as well.

God never did intend that life should be primarily leisure. He intended that life should be primarily work. "Six days a week are for your daily duties and your regular work, but the seventh day is a day of Sabbath rest . . ." (Exodus 20:9,10 TLB). Mary, age 15½, is a little concerned that her busy life limits the time she can spend with her boyfriend. She is busy day and night with school, homework, helping at home, a part-time job, and volunteer work. She sees her boyfriend Tom, age 16, at school each day, and phones him once each evening, and he comes and says hello to her briefly at her job at a fast-food outlet. But they date only infrequently, usually for a couple of hours on a Saturday night.

Mary complained to Dad (Tom put her up to it!) about how little time she spent with Tom; so Mary and Dad analyzed how much time Mary and Tom were together in an average week: fourteen hours! They would have spent much more time together except that Mary's work and activities and Tom's work and activities reduced or counterbalanced their time together.

Mary and Tom had other important activities in their lives besides each other. These activities kept them apart to a reasonable degree. That is the proper counterbalancing role of work. Love develops more deeply and more wisely from these many, small amounts of time spent together over a long period than it develops when love is the sole focus for a brief period. Parents are wise when they encourage their teens to pursue a wide range of work-related activities, so that these teens can maintain their own equilibrium between the proper roles of work and love.

# PART THREE

## Help
## Your
## Adolescents

Parents need to do two things: first, understand their teens, and second, help them. Understanding adolescents is only a means of helping them more effectively. Having understood adolescence as a part of God's perfect, unfolding, creative work, and having understood the teenager's need for personal identity, emotional freedom, romantic love, and satisfying work, let us now move on to *help them*.

Let us look in depth at ways to:

1. *Teach them*—family values about how to treat parents; teach them once more about sex and alert them to the dangers of alcohol, tobacco, and drugs.
2. *Accept them—conditionally.*
3. *Confront them—biblically.*
4. *Release them—lovingly.*

These four aspects of *helping* should give balance and direction to a wholesome parent-teen relationship. With this combination of understanding and helping, we will be well on the way to our goal, which is to *enjoy them—frequently.*

# 7

# Teach Your Teen—
# Thoroughly

Parents are the real teachers. What do parents teach? Everything, but, especially, they teach *the four parts of character:*

1. Values
2. Beliefs
3. Habits
4. Attitudes

These four elements of character are the most fundamental aspects of being a person.

Parents teach in all of the important ways. First, they teach by example. This means they demonstrate "in living color" the values and beliefs, habits and attitudes they wish their adolescents to learn. Second, parents teach directly by "on the job" training; that is, they instruct, reward, exhort, and correct their adolescents in direct, one-to-one, personal exchanges. Remember, though, that the lecture method is the worst method of teaching if it is your only method, or if you use it too often. Third, parents organize and structure the family life and environment to be consistent with what they are trying to teach.

***When do parents teach?*** Parents teach whenever there is opportunity to teach:

1. *Better Sooner Than Later*. Adolescence is not the best time to start to teach; early childhood and middle childhood are better times to start to prepare adolescents for what is ahead, by instilling those helpful aspects of character so important for adult endurance and stability.

2. *Better Late Than Never*. If, for some reason, we *didn't* start teaching our children until they arrived at adolescence, or if we couldn't start teaching them before adolescence, there is still time to start now. It is never too late to begin. There is always hope, even if the situation is more difficult when we start later. No matter how firmly entrenched are certain bad habits and wrong attitudes in our teenagers, we have no choice but to start teaching as soon as we have opportunity. No matter how bad the situation is in your household or family, make a wise assessment, develop a good strategy, get help if you need it, and begin to teach your teenagers—being sure to major on the four parts of character, which are values, beliefs, habits, and attitudes.

3. *Best of all—Sooner and Later*. Many of you taught your children in their infancy, and you kept right on teaching your children as they grew through the stages of childhood. This is the ideal. At this point, your children are no longer children; they are adolescents. Your teaching task now is more difficult because they naturally resist your influence. But your ongoing responsibility is to continue to teach as opportunity presents itself, as long as you sense there is the possibility of being helpful in their development.

4. Shall we leave to the schools the vital task of teaching character? No, the schools have their hands full with the three Rs. Let parents and church communities work a labor of love to develop in their children and adolescents the sound values, true

beliefs, good habits, and right attitudes that are the four parts of good character.

5. Finally, it must be said: "prepare them thoroughly." A thorough preparation will withstand the hard knocks that are surely coming, when peers and the media attempt to ensnare adolescents in a trap of wrong values and false beliefs that could destroy them.

## Teach Them About Sex

Russell and Monica always answered honestly their children's questions about sex. When their 4-year-old son Gabriel was fascinated with Monica's pregnancy, the questions came frequently. By the time Gabriel started first grade, he already had basic sex information. But Gabriel had more than just sex information; Russell and Monica were already sharing with Gabriel their own sexual attitudes and sexual values:

1. Sex is natural and necessary.
2. Sex is enjoyable.
3. Sex is private.
4. Sex is for marriage.

By sharing sexual attitudes and values with Gabriel during his childhood, Russell and Monica were preparing him well for adolescence.

Adolescents handle their own sexuality best when they are prepared in advance for their sexual maturity. This preparation should include sex information and should also major on sexual values and attitudes. Preadolescents should read and study suitable books and pamphlets about sex that are medically accurate and which reflect what parents believe about sexual values and standards.

But no matter what preparation occurs in advance of adolescence, there will still be anxiety, fear, and apprehension in teens about their own sexual development. Menstruation, masturbation, nocturnal emissions, homosexuality, size and shape of sex organs, dating, kissing, petting, premarital sex, teenage pregnancy, abortion, and rape are just a few topics that concern adolescents. Parents must be alert to opportunities to talk about each of these topics with their teenagers, or parents and their adolescents will lose the battle by default. What battle? The battle of conflicting sexual values rages daily on television, radio talk shows, and in the newspapers.

North American society in the sixties and seventies rebelled against the traditional, biblical, Christian values about sex, marriage, and the family. By the mid-eighties, a quarter of a million single, teenaged women were becoming pregnant annually, and more and more teens were becoming sexually active.

Parents need to help teens to understand the dangers of adolescent sexual activity. Parents must recognize that teens need to *think* about sex, and teens must have opportunity to learn to enjoy the company of opposite-sexed peers. But sexual activity for adolescents is both wrong and unwise. Adolescence is a time to prepare for sex, and to anticipate sex, but it is not yet time to participate. Think of the three sub-stages of adolescence:

1. *Early adolescence* is no time for sex; it is the time to search for our own personal identity.
2. *Middle adolescence* is no time for sex; it is the time to pursue emotional freedom from parents.
3. *Later adolescence* is no time for sex; it is the time to pursue romantic attachments in a series of young loves that gradually teach teens about the nature of love and the meaning of commitment.

When is the time for sex? *Adulthood*, within marriage, is the only wise time for sex.

Some parents may be surprised to learn that the majority of adolescents agree that sex should come, not now, but later! Not only do they believe this, but it is the usual practice. In a recent study of middle-class high school boys, tenth grade students averaged only one date in all of their sophomore year! The eleventh grade students averaged one date per month, and a small minority of these were becoming sexually active. Twelfth grade students, on the other hand, were dating regularly, and a minority were sexually active.*

In similar studies of adolescent girls, the dating patterns vary greatly from community to community, but they show that adolescent sexual activity is the exception, not the rule. It is in those areas of the country and community where sexual values have changed that teenagers are following this value change with behavior change, and are pursuing sexual activity more frequently. This value change is not in the best interests of the adolescents themselves, and parents should resist the change vigorously.

What additional steps do you as a parent need to take in teaching your children and teens about sex? Are you doing all you can do? Are you opposing directly the false societal values that can damage the mind and corrupt the thinking of your adolescents? Are you fighting back against the media conspirators who want to lead your teenagers away from Christian sexual values? Teaching facts, values, and attitudes is your responsibility as a parent. *Tuum est*—it is entirely up to you! Do not be passive! Do not be fatalistic! Morals determine sexual behavior, and you are therefore teaching morals as a way of helping your teen to resist current sexual trends.

* Study was done in 1985 in Selkirk, Manitoba, by the counseling department of the high school.

## Marijuana's Unpublicized Dangers

Thirty million North Americans are using marijuana at least occasionally. Almost all of these users are under age 30, and *10 million of these users are under the age of 18!* Most of these users are under the illusion that marijuana is harmless, that it is relaxing, and that it calms the nerves. Nothing could be further from the truth.

What are the facts about marijuana? These striking scientific facts point to the serious harmfulness of marijuana, especially to the brain and reproductive organs.

1. Marijuana is a mild hypnotic-sedative and influences the mind by sedating and slowing down thinking. It reduces reaction time, alertness, and concentration, leaving the mind numb, suggestible, lethargic, and inefficient.

2. Marijuana is not a narcotic. There is no evidence of physical dependence in humans. Quite a number of years ago, a very rich man used his power and influence to get the World Health Organization to classify marijuana as a narcotic, but it is not. It is a mild hypnotic-sedative that does not produce chemical dependence.

*The danger of dependence with marijuana is psychological dependence.* Any person who has the slightest tendency to procrastinate about problems, deny reality, or lose his willpower can easily become entangled in the dreamlike, never-never land of the marijuana trance. The marijuana stupor confuses reality, leads us to rebel against reason, and minimizes the sense of responsibility.

3. *Marijuana damages the brain,* especially the limbic system of the brain and the hypothalamus, resulting in flattened emotions. In the case of long-term marijuana users, there are not just flattened emotions, there are virtually no emotions left at all. Even one-billionth of a gram of THC—the active hallucinogen in

marijuana—affects the hypothalamus and disrupts its work of producing the correct visceral or "gut" reaction to suit each behavior.[+]

4. *Marijuana damages the reproductive organs.* Marijuana is harmful to males. Only one month of regular smoking of marijuana damages the testicles, resulting in lowered sperm count, decrease in sperm mobility, increase in the percentage of deformed sperm, fewer orgasms, flat orgasms, lower rate of sexual activity, lower level of sexual interest, and lower level of the male hormone testosterone.[‡]

Marijuana is harmful to females, in that it suppresses hormones that control the proper function of the ovaries. Women on even moderate amounts of marijuana show a decrease in prolactin, a hormone that is important in milk production. A significantly high percentage of babies of mothers who are marijuana users show signs of nervous system abnormalities. Even two marijuana cigarettes per week of the mild Mexican and American types of marijuana produce negative effects in the offspring. Even one marijuana cigarette per week of the much stronger Jamaican and Colombian varieties is harmful to offspring.[§]

In summary, marijuana use in this generation is an epidemic and a disaster. Your teens and your younger children need to consider these questions seriously: Do you want to have your wits about you? Do you want to be a motivated person? Do you want to preserve your ability to respond with vibrant and appropriate emotions? Then do not use marijuana! Do not even try it: it is a loser's way downhill. Marijuana does not relax, it sedates. Marijuana is not good for your nerves; it numbs them into senselessness.

[+] Alexander Jacuboric, University of British Columbia.
[‡] Dr. Wylie Hembree, Columbia University College of Physicians and Surgeons.
[§] Dr. Peter Fried, Psychology Department, Carleton University.

If your children and adolescents are trapped in the marijuana mess, share these pages with them.

## Alcohol

Alcohol is the nightmare that never goes away. Alcohol, like marijuana, is also a mild hypnotic-sedative. One bottle of beer raises blood alcohol to 15 mg/100 ml and produces visual and muscle impairment for one hour. For this reason, Sweden has set the minimum legal blood alcohol level for Swedish drivers at 10 mg/100 ml. What is the legal blood alcohol level in your area?

Because 83 percent of vehicle accidents are alcohol-related, Sweden has a minimum fine for drinking drivers of $5,000. What is the minimum fine for drinking drivers in your area? In Sweden, drinking drivers automatically lose their driver's license for *life*, and there is no appeal and no review! What is the minimum period of license suspension for drinking drivers in your area? In Sweden there is a minimum term of imprisonment for drinking drivers of one year in jail. What is the period of minimum imprisonment in your area? In Sweden there are many alcoholics but there are *no drinking drivers*.

Are there drinking drivers in your area? Could you do something about it? The family, financial, employment, health, and social problems of alcohol use make alcohol the number one nightmare that never goes away. Alcohol use is a major cause of ineffective anxiety. Alcohol causes all of life to sour, decay, and disintegrate.

## Teach Them to Treat You Like Royalty

With the cautionary teaching about sex, drugs, and alcohol completed, we turn to the more positive teaching about family relationships.

Do you expect your adolescents to treat you well? Then teach them how. Don't just tell them; teach them. The big difference between *telling* and *teaching* is that teaching is a planned learning process, which is what adolescents need—a carefully planned learning program to teach them exactly how you wish them to treat you.

Do you teach your adolescents how to treat you? Remember that repetition is the best teacher. Teach the same lessons as often as necessary until you are getting results.

Your teaching should focus on answering (in their minds) the following questions:

*1. How well should teenagers treat parents?*   Answer: like royalty, with love, kindness, consideration, respect, courtesy, and appreciation. In a word, they should treat you well, and their adolescent years should be *for you* years of enjoyment because you are so pleased and happy to be an object of their love and respect.

If you are being treated unfairly, unkindly, and without respect, you must make an honest, accurate evaluation of your family situation and find out what needs to be changed in you and in your adolescents. Then make those changes. If you need outside help to improve the parent-teen relationship, then get that help. Remember, they are no longer children, so the parent-child relationship is over and done with. They are adolescents, and they need a parent-adolescent relationship.

Do not waste time pondering the many reasons *why* your adolescent is not treating you well. "Why" questions are not usually helpful because they drag us into the past as we try to analyze our own complicated history. The background of every parent-adolescent relationship is less significant than we think, because yesterday is gone forever. Today and all the tomorrows are what should concern us, and that is the reason "how" questions, and "what" questions are more useful than "why" questions to help us improve today and prepare for tomorrow.

Examples of good "how" questions:

- How can I, the parent, manage my own behavior so that I *merit the respect* of my teenagers?
- How can I motivate my teens to treat me well?
- How can I make my points so that they understand and appreciate my need to be treated well?

Examples of good "what" questions:

- What do I need to change in me?
- What do they need to change in their habits, attitudes, priorities, and beliefs?

**2. What is the language of respect?**   Notice that we stick with questions of *how* and *what*. The first concern should be the language of adolescent-parent communications. Language is important because when language is right, thinking tends to change for the better.

Parents should teach the language of respect by their own example in parent-to-adolescent communication, but they should also teach by direct training, instruction, correction, praise, and reward. Bob and Charlotte use the language of respect, and they expect their adolescents to use it too. They do not accept any instances of disrespectful language. Nor do they punish harshly, but their adolescents are careful about how they address Mom and Dad. They know that if they make even one poor choice of a word or even one hint of a disrespectful tone of voice, the result is a precise and effective teaching session on what is acceptable language.

Their daughter Elsa, age 13, is a master of subtle insults, snide remarks, double-meaning barbs, put-downs, and insinuations, but she saves these types of disrespectful language for peers, not for her parents. She knows her parents will address the situation *fully* each time she uses such language. She knows they will insist on a full conference immediately to find a way to prevent a recurrence of disrespectful language. At such conferences, parents are united in a powerful expression of sincere hurt and disappointment, and they make an effective presentation for mutual respect in language as the basis of the parent-adolescent relationship.

Elsa has been involved in such conferences before and knows now that Mom and Dad are both right and fair. Thus she exercises verbal self-control, which means using terms that recognize and honor her parents' rightful position and their immeasurable contribution to her life. They are terms of endearment and respect using normal English, not her peer-group lingo. It involves *the use of serious language,* not flippant speech. (Elsa once said, "Hey, Daddy-O," and she and Dad had a little chuckle, but she understood clearly afterward that such phrases must only be the exception, not the rule.) Bob and Charlotte permit no threats, no exaggerations, no deceptions, no lies, no accusations, no nagging, no harassment.

No wonder Bob and Charlotte enjoy their daughter most of the time! No wonder their daughter enjoys herself and her parents; she knows where she stands and can get on with the pursuit of identity, individuality, and independence. About one-half of all parent-adolescent relationships are as enjoyable as the relationships in this family, and the other half are working toward it. The work of building good parent-adolescent relationships is a step-by-step process, not an all-at-once process. So focus not on how much farther you have to go, but on making the next step wisely.

*3. What is the language of appreciation?*    Wendy is a mother who expects a "thank you" when she does things for others. She doesn't expect wages or returned favors, just a sincere "thank you.'' If she passes the bread or salt during supper, she expects a "thank you.'' If she washes the clothes, she expects thanks from those who wear them. She is so serious about thank-yous that she teaches the importance of the word. She also likes "Yes, please,'' and her family has developed the firm habit of saying please and thank you as a result of her insistence.

Wendy is so determined about the language of appreciation that she makes extreme efforts to teach her adolescents that the expression of appreciation is mandatory. She used to have frequent, hot arguments with her son Mike, age 17, because Mike was taking her for granted. Wendy does not intend for anyone to take her kindness for granted; so when Mike did so, she went on strike: no more privileges, favors, or services rendered for Mike for a set period of time. Mike dramatically expressed his anger and disgust the first few times Wendy went on strike, but Wendy stuck to her guns, and made her points to Mike over and over, as strongly and as wisely as she could. When Mike saw that she was not going to accept his uncaring, macho-man attitude, he gradually came around to full use of the language of appreciation. And, as often happens, when his language and manner changed, Mike's attitude also improved.

**4. When parents say no and teens are upset, what can teens say and do that is acceptable?**   They can *argue* the point until the parents have listened as much as they wish to listen. The adolescents can "haggle"; that is, they can bargain and make counter-proposals to their parents until the parents have listened as much as they wish to listen. But teenagers cannot threaten, insult, nag, or hassle their parents.

Are you teaching your teenager the language of respect, common courtesy, and appreciation? Are you being treated like royalty by your adolescents? If not, don't just tell them how you wish them to treat you, *teach them.*

# 8

# Accept Your Teen— Conditionally

Jack was so upset with his daughter Susan, age 15, that he couldn't speak to her for a day and a half. She had spoken to him in an ignorant and thoughtless manner, and it so hurt and disappointed him that he had to avoid her until he figured out how to respond to her. Jack and his wife, Louise, had a number of private talks about Susan, and Jack used these talks to drain some of the hurt out of his system. Then, when he was ready, he sat Susan down and talked to her. These are the points he tried to make:

*Point 1.* "Susan, you said some horrible things to me. Someone else didn't say them, you did. I have to accept this fact. Your mind and your inner self reacted to frustration and disappointment by responding in this way to me. I accept the fact that this is the way you were thinking and feeling. As I think about your age, your personality, and the pressures you are experiencing, I can understand why you felt and acted the way you did."

*Point 2.* "But don't do it again! Smarten up. Thinking and feeling are one thing—you may think or feel as you wish, but do not put these thoughts and feelings into words as you did the other day. Find an acceptable way to express your frustrations and disappointments. I don't accept what you said to me, and I don't want it to recur."

*Point 3.* "Most of the time you speak with respect and courtesy. Thanks for all the times when you talk to me kindly. I always appreciate every kind word."

*Point 4.* "When you have unacceptable words on the tip of your tongue, bite it! Families can only survive if each member bridles his or her tongue, exercising care in the way they all express themselves to each other.

"As a member of this family, you have the opportunity to bless us or hurt us. When you talk to us in horrible ways, it is like putting a knife to the throat of this family. Families can be destroyed; the fabric of family life can be torn to shreds by unkindness and wrong language. Therefore, think before you speak."

*Point 5.* "I do not wish to punish you or threaten you because we should be able to work out our family problems without that. But I do want to forewarn you that you must find a way to stop this kind of behavior. If you don't stop, then I will try to find ways to stop it."

As Jack made each of these points, Susan was listening and making points of her own to Jack. Then it was Jack's turn to listen. The end of their dialogue was an understanding and appreciation by Susan that her father could accept her feelings and thoughts as being her present frame of mind, but he couldn't accept her ignorant and thoughtless choice of words.

She felt his love and acceptance as his daughter, and she felt her acceptance as a full member of the family. At the same time she felt her father's rejection of that part of her—her unacceptable language—that had resulted in the silent treatment she had subsequently received from him.

Teens need acceptance, and Susan felt the actual extent of her father's acceptance, while at the same time appreciating its limits. Father had done well in communicating to her that acceptance must be tied to reality: we accept the acceptable, and we reject the unacceptable; that is all we can possibly do. There is no hidden, unknowable mystery about acceptance: acceptance is simply an open, honest reflection of our evaluation of the relationship. Jack's acceptance, and his rejection, was the real state of their relationship as Jack was experiencing it.

Susan had a choice when Jack rejected her. She could keep right on dishing out more horrible language, or she could change her way of speaking so that it would be acceptable to Jack. She chose to listen, and what she heard helped her decide to change. It is a credit both to Jack and Susan that together they could act (Susan's bad language), react (Jack's initial silence and his confrontation with Susan), dialogue, and finally restore mutual acceptance. Their acceptance and rejection of each other see-sawed up and down as they attempted to be honest with each other. Acceptance was the goal toward which both were working, but honest rejection identified the problem area to be resolved.

Let us compare acceptance and rejection:

| ACCEPTANCE | REJECTION |
|---|---|
| • Acceptance is a favorable response in which we willingly receive the other person. | • Rejection finds something wrong in the relationship that cannot be ignored. |

| ACCEPTANCE | REJECTION |
|---|---|
| • Acceptance welcomes the other person, listens, and gives the benefit of the doubt. | • Rejection is a message to let the other person know about wrongs. |
| • Acceptance focuses on good points about the other person. | • Rejection insists that something wrong is hurting the relationship. |
| • Acceptance makes comments about good points. | |
| • Acceptance encourages and appreciates. | • Rejection invites the other person to change and/or explore the possibility of change. |
| • Acceptance is hopeful and looks forward to growth and improvement in the other person. | |
| • Acceptance recognizes progress, and notes if the other person is making even one small step in the right direction. | |
| • Acceptance does *not* wink at sin, unfairness, or unkindness. | |

With your adolescent, you should strive for a balance of acceptance and rejection that reflects reality. But because reality shifts, your acceptance and rejection will change frequently too. Acceptance is a continuously changing, shifting, responsive process, and so is rejection.

At times acceptance will dominate in the parent-adolescent relationship, and this indicates a peaceful period. How easy it is to be accepting when they are lovable, courteous, considerate, and helpful! But acceptance is a balancing of love, reality, and justice.

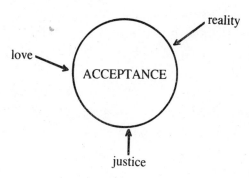

What the parent or teen finds acceptable today may not be the same tomorrow.

Do not work at being accepting. It should come naturally. The only exception is a parent who is hypercritical, suspicious, negative, cynical, hoping to catch the other person off base, spoiling the other person's genuine attempt to improve. If you are this negative parent, you need to make a special effort to be accepting. However, the great majority of parents should trust their spontaneous reactions—whether of acceptance or rejection—because their minds are continually evaluating the parent-teen relationship, and acceptance or rejection is simply their expression of their evaluation. Parents, have confidence in your ability to evaluate: you know what is good and fair, so if you like what you see in your adolescent, express it.

Do not work at being rejecting. It should also come naturally. The only exception here is a parent who is a passive, long-suffering, inhibited, timid person. If you are this passive, timid parent, then work at being more rejecting. You are probably not rejecting enough, so your goal is to try harder to address the negatives of the relationship. However, most parents can say what needs to be said about the negatives. Rejecting, when done wisely, is very hard work, and parents earn their spurs when they speak up and deal with whatever they believe is unfair or unkind behavior by their adolescent.

The goal, of course, is a proper balance of acceptance and rejection that reflects the real need of the relationship at the particular time. Continuous appraisal and reflection should bring that balance.

## Acceptance Is Conditional

Acceptance is conditional. The limit we place on acceptance is our refusal to accept anything that goes against our minimum requirements of morality and justice in relationships. Acceptance reflects our view of morality and justice, and Susan could count on her father's acceptance if she treated him well. *If* is a big word that implies choice. Susan's choice of language and behavior would determine her father's acceptance of her. It was entirely up to her; she had the choice.

Adolescents need acceptance. Their bodies and minds are growing so quickly that they can hardly keep pace with their own growth. They need acceptance as a reflection of how others view their progress. How does acceptance work?

Acceptance is an honest response to the strengths and good qualities of others. Acceptance evaluates the relationship, and focuses on positives without denying negatives. We have a positive regard, a good feeling, a YES response, a hopeful attitude about the relationship. It is as though we are saying, "I am on your side, and I want what's best for you, and I find many things desirable about the relationship."

Acceptance is always conditional. We all have our standards about how relationships should be, and we must reject (not accept) those aspects of the relationship that are immoral, unkind, or unjust.

Ellen loves her 13-year-old daughter Dawn, but is furious when Dawn charges expensive, long-distance calls to Ellen's phone number. This action of Dawn's is unacceptable, and Ellen doesn't accept it. But the very way in which the unacceptance is expressed leaves the door wide open for Dawn to regain her mother's acceptance. Here again the choice is Dawn's; if she wants to regain her mother's acceptance, she knows what to do.

Acceptance is a positive regard, but it is not *unconditional* positive regard. We first look at our teenagers *objectively*, not positively or negatively, and we call their behavior as we see it. We label their behavior clearly so there can be no doubt or confusion about what is acceptable and what is unacceptable. By making the labels clear, we do our teens a great favor. They then know exactly how we evaluate the relationship, and it is up to them to respond and change if they wish to regain our acceptance.

Each parent must have his or her own limits of tolerance for immoral, unkind, and unjust behavior. Our adolescents need to know what those limits are. We need to communicate them clearly, and we need to spell out what our teens must do to regain our goodwill and our willingness to cooperate in helping ways.

Brad, age 15, is confused and resentful because of problems with his older brother. Unfortunately, his confusion about his brother made him lash out at his parents. His parents understand the situation and appreciate that Brad is presently his own worst self. But they also know that Brad has many good years ahead of him, and they know that he will make lots of progress in those years ahead. Brad's parents do not accept his unkind actions toward them, and they tell him so. But they leave the door open because they love him, and because they see so many positive signs of the kind of man he will become. Their acceptance is open-ended: it allows for Brad to change, to grow, and to move ahead. His parents are positive because they are hopeful; where there is life, there is hope.

Brad's parents accept his confusion and resentment. What does it mean to accept his confusion? This means they listen to his confusion and try to understand his feelings without hurrying to make suggestions. Suggestions can come later. The parents also accept Brad's resentment. What does it mean to accept his resentment? This means that they seek to understand these feelings as coming from Brad's inner self, and the parents accept the resentments as part of Brad's real inner self. They listen to Brad's reasons for his resentments and they accept them as his reasons. They do NOT accept his reasons as logical or adequate ones. They simply accept them as Brad's reasons—as reasons that appear logical and adequate to Brad. They try to appreciate his reasons from his point of view, and their acceptance of him acknowledges that this is where Brad's mind is right now.

Are you able to accept confusion and resentments, weaknesses and deficits of character without accepting the wrong behavior that results from them? Perhaps for you this is too fine a line to draw, but with adolescents it is important to draw this line. Yes, be accepting of all their weaknesses and confusion and deficits. But do not accept wrong behaviors that flow from these weaknesses of character. Your adolescents need your disapproval! They will have more willpower, more resistance to temptation, more desire to do good if you stand firmly for what you believe is good and fair.

## Accept Their Adolescence

*Early adolescence* is the identity search that helps adolescents to be different, especially different from their parents. Can you accept their need to be different? When they are developing different interests from your own, when their personalities are becoming unique and individual, can you accept their need to be different from you?

*Middle adolescence* is the time when they need *not to be needed* by parents. They do not want you to need their love, concern, time, and energy. They need your life to be full *without them* so that they can, without guilt, begin gradually to push you away. This is their time to achieve emotional independence from you. The tie of emotional dependency must be broken. Can you as a parent *accept* this hard fact, and can you accept them in this new way? Can you accept their need not to need you and their need not to be needed *by* you?

*Later adolescence* is a time when opposite-sexed peers become more important than parents. At this time, parents are often running a distant second. Can you accept them as they give their hearts to someone else?

Accept these three sub-stages of adolescence and the special adolescent needs that are unique to each of these stages. Then you will truly be accepting your adolescents.

## Repentance Restores Acceptance

"I'm sorry, Mom. I shouldn't have done it, and it will not happen again," says Charlotte, age 12, and these magic words of repentance indicate a change of mind and heart. Mother forgives, and the hurt and disappointment are replaced by acceptance.

But forgiveness comes more slowly for the father of Kevin, age 16. "I'm sorry, Dad. This has happened quite a few times before, and I'm sorry it has happened again. The next time I will simply get up and leave if I see there are drugs and alcohol present." Father says to himself, "Is this the real thing? Is Kevin genuinely sorry or is he just saying the words? He has said the same things before, and the words meant nothing then. Does he mean it this time? Has he really had a change of mind and heart, or is he just deceiving me?'' If Father sees a real change of behavior in the following weeks, then he will know there was a real change of mind. Kevin's father tells it straight to Kevin, "We want to believe you, but we must wait to see if your actions change. Let us help you if we can, but it is mainly up to you. In the meantime, Kevin, no more use of the car for you until we see a real change.''

Can you as a parent balance out the need for acceptance with the need for real repentance when your adolescent has violated certain aspects of the mutual understanding between you both? The principle of biblical repentance requires that you withhold acceptance until there is evidence of a real change of heart. Repentance does have a marvelous restorative effect on a relationship, but the repentance must be genuine. Use these principles of repentance in parenting:

*1. If no repentance, then no forgiveness.* There is no limit—not even seventy times seven (Matthew 18:22)—to the number of times a parent should forgive his teenager *provided* there is repentance from his teen first. In such instances, the Christian parent must be willing to forgive, over and over and over. But if there is no repentance, then even once is too many times to forgive. Why is repentance necessary? Because forgiveness without repentance would mean that the forgiver accepts the wrongdoing as being right!

*2. Repentance is not sorrow for sins.* Godly sorrow is commendable and desirable, but it is different from repentance. Godly sorrow in New Testament Greek is *metamelomai*, but the Greek word for repentance is *metanoia*, which means not sorrow but a change of mind and conduct. As a parent, do not be fooled by expressions of sorrow for wrongdoing. Sorrow is not repentance, and repentance is not sorrow. Repentance means that there is a real change of mind and heart, and genuine repentance *always* results in a change of behavior. "Prove your repentance by the fruit . . . it bears" (Matthew 3:8 NEB). To test whether your teenager is sincere, you may have to wait and see if there is a real change of behavior. Teenagers need to know that real change on their part is the price of parental acceptance.

*3. Do not wait for perfection.*    Adolescents, with their new hormones, new brain power, and inexperience, often stagger and reel from one difficulty and offense to another. If parents waited for them to get their whole act together before granting acceptance, acceptance would never come. So, in the middle of teenagers' offenses and assorted unacceptable behavior, parents must look for, recognize, praise, and accept what they see as even the slightest progress. Always be looking for something good to say that reflects your acceptance of that part of their behavior.

"Don't throw out the baby with the dirty bathwater!" Don't give up hope because things are going wrong. Don't reject the good along with the bad. Sort it out, and respond with acceptance to all that is good.

*4. Be a stickler most of the time, but realize that there is also a time to be patient and ease off ever so slightly.*    Read the signs and remember that unusual conditions at home or in a teen's own life often call for unusual understanding and a gentle spirit on the part of the parent.

## Acceptance Is Christ's Way

Jesus dealt directly with people in genuine, transparent honesty. He expressed both acceptance and rejection depending on the state of each person's mind and heart. But His goal was to accept them, not reject them. He always made it clear to people that if He did reject them, it was because of their own attitude or behavior. The door was forever open to them to come and receive His acceptance, provided they were repentant.

When Christ rejects, what is the door to His acceptance? Repentance. It is for this reason we have discussed repentance at length. Christ accepts everyone, regardless of the wickedness or ignorance or confusion of mind and conduct, if there is genuine repentance. Sinners of all kinds, without exception, can come to Him in repentance and receive forgiveness and eternal life.

In what way does this encouraging theology of Christian acceptance relate to parenting, especially the Christian parenting of adolescents? Christ is the Christian parent's example in acceptance. From Christ and the New Testament, parents can find all they need to know about how to accept their teenagers. But parents beware, because the Christian standard is not society's standard, and the Christian way is not the easiest way for parents or adolescents. Yet Christ's way is the best way because it gives the best results in the long run. It restructures the family so that parents and their teenagers can enjoy each other most of the time.

What are the important features of Christian acceptance? How does Christian acceptance apply to families and adolescents?

*Christian acceptance is a message.*    Jewish leaders hated and despised the adulteress, and they wanted Jesus to condemn her. But Jesus looked and saw a heart of genuine repentance, and He said, "I do not condemn you . . . go, and sin no more" (*see* John 8:11). Acceptance sends a message—with words, tone of voice, facial expression, and posture—that says we can receive the other person willingly and favorably in our mind and our life. Acceptance says that we can set aside the past and we can receive and welcome the other person *as is*. Acceptance does not condemn, it challenges ("Go, and sin no more"). Acceptance does not criticize, complain, nag, belittle, or degrade; acceptance looks for the good and recognizes and encourages it.

*Christian acceptance is approval of the person's present frame of mind,* but is not approval of past sins.    Nothing can change the past, but a Christian parent can forgive the past if an adolescent's present frame of mind is right. That is the focus of Christian acceptance, namely, *the present state of mind of the other person.* What is the present attitude? What is the present moral outlook? What is the present purpose and the present intention? Parents make a great mistake if they focus on the past, because the past is never a reliable indicator of the present state of mind of an adolescent or any other person.

# 9

# Confront Your Teen— Biblically

Any fool can start a war, but the purpose of this chapter is to help families avoid them. Families need constructive confrontation; they do not need war.

Let us be very clear about the differences between confrontation and war:

| | CONFRONTATION | WAR |
|---|---|---|
| Main feature | A face-to-face verbal encounter to resolve a conflict of ideas and interests. | A struggle to defeat, control, and enslave another person. |
| Process | Present facts and use reason to try to win over the other person. | Present threats, punishments, injuries to force the other person to submit. |
| Choice | Leave the choice to the other person. | Leave no choice to the other person. |
| Means | Appeal to reality, to reason, and to sound values. | Give an ultimatum to obey or pay the penalty. |

| | CONFRONTATION | WAR |
|---|---|---|
| Results | Both sides win with a mutually acceptable compromise of action. | There are both winners and losers, and lingering animosity. |
| Effect on Families | Helps family members appreciate each other's point of view, and strengthens families. | Destroys families, causes deep wounds of hatred and distrust. |

Is there ever a legitimate situation in which parents must go to war against their own children and teenagers? Definitely, there is. Any time that children or adolescents refuse to reason or negotiate, and instead resort to actions that parents know to be destructive to the family, parents must use force, threats, and punishment until the children and the adolescents change their ways. This is war, and the children or adolescents are the aggressors who must be stopped.

It is to be hoped that this sort of warfare takes place when children are young. The parents pursue the war justly and swiftly, and there are hurt feelings, but no lasting injuries. The family recovers and moves forward. The finest Christian parents in the world have gone to war—regretfully, lovingly, and promptly—when they knew it had to be done. But even as these parents warred, they knew that lasting peace only comes from winning the other person over, not by winning battles, and not by forcing the other person to live by our rules. War, as drastic and costly as it is, is a short-term measure only. Wise parents choose constructive confrontation as the only sure foundation for joyful family life.

Wars between parents and adolescents are more dangerous and damaging to families than wars against children. Adolescents are bigger, and the result is bigger wars. Teens are smarter, more persistent, more capable of surviving without the family's help, so parent-adolescent wars run a greater risk of permanently disrupting and destroying families. This is why confrontation is the better way. Confrontation may be long, loud, emotional, and frustrating, but it is much to be preferred over war because the result is voluntary cooperation within the family.

## Confronting Is Christian and Biblical

Jesus confronted people. For example, He confronted James and John about their excessive personal ambition. First, in His own mind, Jesus made the decision not to let the problem ride. The beginning of confrontation is always the decision to confront. The relationship between Jesus and the two apostles was getting out of focus because of a serious conflict of values. Jesus' decision to confront was a decision to bring this conflict of values out in the open, to inspect it, to look at the facts that supported the conflicting states of mind, to deal with the conflict, and attempt to resolve it. The purpose of confronting is always the attempt to resolve the conflict.

Second, Jesus selected a time and place for the confrontation. He waited until their own jealousies had produced a deadlock. Then He spoke to them face-to-face and said in so many words, "Let's look at all the facts and see if we can agree on a way through this impasse." Then, by an appeal to reality, to reason, and to sound values, He reasoned with them to *change their minds*. That is the ultimate goal of confrontation: not merely a change of words or even a change of actions, but a change of mind and heart. That is the biblical view of repentance. Then the new values and attitudes of a changed mind and heart will properly resolve the conflict.

Jesus could have arranged a pleasant picnic at the beach.

Instead He chose to confront, because it is the Christian and biblical way. You don't stick your head in the sand. You don't wear rose-colored glasses. You face reality, including the conflicts within relationships. Then, in a just and skillful way, you directly confront those around you on the matters that are important to you.

The apostle Paul was an effective confronter. He honestly faced the conflicts in relationships and sought face-to-face, verbal encounters to bring about an end to conflict.

Christian parents are acting in a Christian and biblical manner when they decide to confront their teens on important conflicts of values. The process of confrontation may be unpleasant and exhausting, but it is the moral and responsible thing to do.

## Confronting Is Essential in Families

Why is confronting essential in families? First, it is essential because family members cannot read one another's minds. If a family member is frustrated, angry, disappointed, ashamed, or sorrowful about a relationship with another family member, that frustrated person must speak up and say what is on his mind. Two minds have a chance to come together on a subject if they know each other's whys and wherefores, but in silence they can only remain apart.

So family members must speak up. They must speak the truth as they see it. Paul says, "Speak the truth in love" (*see* Ephesians 4:15). A face-to-face, verbal encounter makes a new understanding possible if it is handled wisely. Parents ought not to suffer in silence; they must speak the truth in love. Of course, this goes equally for the teenagers in the family; they must also speak up and do their best to persuade their parents of the rightness and fairness of their point of view.

Second, confronting is essential in families because change and growth in family members requires new and different commitments. Adolescence is a period of rapid physical and intellectual growth, and such rapid growth requires regular changes in commitments.

Adolescence has four milestones of growth: (1) a new identity as a person, (2) the need for emotional freedom, (3) the need for romantic love and peer relationships, and (4) the need for meaningful employment. As each of these milestones is reached, the adolescent is a changed person, and his new self requires a new relationship to parents. If parents do not accept these changes, they will confront their adolescents in an attempt to turn time backward. The adolescents will also confront their parents in an attempt to be better understood. Accept or confront—these are the alternatives of parents.

In our previous chapter on acceptance, we stressed the fact that acceptance is an either-or situation. The "either" is acceptance, and the "or" is confrontation. Either adolescents accept or confront. Either parents accept or confront. This does not mean that parents should accept everything, nor should adolescents. Confronting is an alternative to be used if we find something about the other person to be unacceptable.

## Get Ready for the Struggle of Your Life

Rose knew five years in advance that her daughter Angela would be a vigorous, determined adolescent who would not take no for an answer. So Rose saved her strength and readied herself for the countless confrontations she expected. Surprise, surprise! The nightmare never happened. When Angela started to push hard at age 12 for extra freedom for which she was not ready, Rose wisely said no. Angela argued, and Rose held her ground, giving good reasons, stating them very clearly, and challenging Angela to act responsibly in order to be given more responsibility.

"Prove to me that you can be trusted, and that you can handle yourself maturely, and I will see about giving you more freedom," said Rose. She said it again when Angela was 14, and later when Angela was 17. Rose was pleased to extend Angela's freedom when Angela demonstrated the ability to handle it. Over the intervening years, Rose was always ready for the struggle of her life, but because she was ready, the struggle was not so strenuous. They did have many lengthy discussions, and they had their share of shouting matches, but Rose's good balance of acceptance and confrontation helped them to work out their differences amicably.

Can you imagine being exhausted for three years and gulping antacids daily just because there is a teenager in the house? Tom's son, Gordon, was a "big mouth" at age 13, knew "everything" at age 14, and at age 15 figured he was Mr. World Winner. Tom's strategy as a Christian father was "accept what is acceptable, try to understand, and confront when necessary."

At least a hundred times over this three-year period, Tom and Gordon stood eyeball-to-eyeball and pleaded, shouted, reasoned, argued, screamed, and discussed until they hammered out an understanding. After each encounter Tom would swallow the antacids, while Gordon would fully recover in seconds! But Tom knew that all of these exhausting struggles were the finest parenting efforts of his life, and they were having good results. Gordon was slowly becoming a man. He was enjoying the slow and steady increase of freedoms and responsibilities, and Tom was proud of the signs of progress.

When Gordon was age 16½, Tom said, "I think you are ready to manage your own life, and come and go as you please. Do you think you could handle this? It would be quite a responsibility, and Mom and I would want you to make us proud. Let's talk about how this could work out.'' As this family worked out the details and made clear the dangers as well as the opportunities, they set in motion a plan for Gordon to monitor his own progress. It was going to be up to him. Eighteen months later, the family celebrated Gordon's successes, and Gordon's 18th birthday party was a symbol of a well-deserved freedom.

It is completely normal for parents and their adolescents to have frequent, fierce confrontations. Congratulations are due those parents and teens who can make these disputes productive* to a good family relationship. Your adolescents' survival and happiness are worth a struggle. Get in there and give it your best effort! They need your views and opinions to counterbalance the false values of peers and of the mass media. They need your love and concern to help them resist a thousand temptations. Do not sit back and passively watch your son's and daughter's minds becoming ensnared in a trap of confusion and sin. Instead, confront them, not with insults and put-downs, but with your wisest reasoning and your clearest communications, to persuade them of why you believe and feel the way you do. Later on, they will love you for confronting them.

## The Whole Purpose of Confronting Is to Win Them Over

Jack wanted obedience from his 16-year-old twin daughters concerning their ten o'clock curfew. He demanded their obedience and never got it. He thought he was confronting, but he was simply ordering and commanding them to obey. The daughters never knew Jack's reasoning for the curfew, so they never could evaluate its wisdom. Because they could not see the reasoning, it was easy for them to reject Jack's demands. Jack should have tried to win them over to his way of thinking. Then if he succeeded, they would have acted differently out of their own change of heart, their own new way of thinking.

Persuasion is the heart of confrontation. Win them over to your values and your way of thinking. Persuade them that your way is wise, fair, and just, and let them make the choice because your values have become their own.

Sure, you can force them to obey for a little longer—perhaps a year or two. Force is necessary and acceptable on occasion if there is a crisis or emergency. But your goal must be to win them over by sound reasoning, so that when the choice is theirs, they will make wise choices on their own.

The pressure, strain, and hard work of the confronting process stem from the difficulty of getting an idea from one mind to another. The person with the idea has that idea in the absolute privacy of his own mind. What an accomplishment to be able to take a private idea and put it into words so that another mind can consider, understand, and accept or reject it!

Study this statement from the National Council of Advertisers:

*"When an idea fails to enter the mind of the receiver, the sole responsibility for that failure lies with the sender."*

This statement puts all the responsibility for communication on one person, the sender. The intended receiver has no responsibility in communication, not even to listen, to consider, or to think.

If you were to accept this statement as your own philosophy, you could use it to formulate an excellent philosophy of confrontation: "When one of my parental ideas fails, for any reason whatever, to enter and be accepted by my teenager's mind, the sole responsibility for that failure lies with me, the parent. When my adolescent does not accept my ideas, I should not blame him, neither should I pout, nor give up and quit trying. Because the idea exists only in my own mind, I have no choice but to try, try, and try again to get the idea across to my adolescent:

- trying by different means,
- trying by different strategies,
- trying at different times,
- trying to get even one small part of the idea across at a time,
- and never giving up."

A final point about winning them over: winning doesn't mean that they lose. There should be no losers in confrontation; both sides win when either side accepts some parts of the other's point of view. So help your teens to see it as a gain for them too. After all, truth is truth, and if they have come one step closer and have discovered some added truth as a result of the confrontation process, then they are winners too.

## Score Points, or Forget the Entire Exercise

You may be saying to yourself, "Confronting is my weakness. I always say the wrong thing in the wrong way at the wrong time. There is no way I could ever confront my adolescents successfully. I was born to suffer quietly, not to confront." Let's examine this statement.

1. "Confronting is my weakness." If this is true and you are in fact a weak confronter, good for you that you can admit it! Facing this weakness honestly is step one on the way to overcoming it.

2. "I always say the wrong thing." Again, admitting this is helpful. The reality of your wrong words needs to be faced so you can improve.

3. "I could never confront my adolescents successfully." Well, how gloomy can we get? Are you a prophet who knows the future? You are probably just a parent who needs some coaching and practice to confront successfully.

4. "I was born to suffer quietly, not to confront." This is not true. We are all born to become the person we choose to become, and we always have the choice to change. For the most part, we choose our own character, beliefs, values, and life-style. When we review our "self" from time to time, we can make such changes as we wish (it's hard work, of course).

We were not born to suffer; we were born to live, to survive, to think, to grow, to mature, to love, to cry—to do all the good things we are capable of doing. But it requires determination to make the decisions and commitments that will help us to become the best we can be. You were not born to suffer, but to grow and to put your hand in God's hand and walk forward with Him into a future of exciting, unlimited possibilities. So walk with Him, away from the stifling hopelessness of fatalism toward the abundant Christian life. Stop thinking you *can't* do it, because of course you *can* do it—with a change of mind and some coaching and practice.

After this Dutch uncle's lecture, you should say to yourself,

"Okay, I won't be fatalistic. I will struggle until I become a skillful confronter."

## Scoring Points Is the Real Basis of Confronting

What does a skillful confronter do? A skillful confronter *scores points* and then helps the other person translate each point into constructive changes in the relationship.

Scoring points means *getting others to see the truth, justice, and wisdom of our point of view*. We have scored a point if the other person sees what we mean and accepts it as valid. Turn the light on in your adolescent's head so he/she can see your point of view. Illuminate your point of view so it becomes acceptable to him or her. Use facts, evidence, truth, reality—whatever is necessary for your teen to appreciate your concerns.

The only legitimate means of scoring points is *sound reason*. Sound reason means we logically organize and express the facts. Then we challenge the other person to deduce from these facts (premises) the same conclusions that these facts imply to us. This reasoning process helps the other person to see that our point of view is not simply personal, but flows logically from a clear understanding of the facts.

At least 50 percent of adolescents have this reasoning ability. They can reason logically, and our task is to give them the facts as we see them and then challenge them to use reason to come to our point of view.

Most parent-adolescent confrontations are a vigorous exchange of values, beliefs, and attitudes. The wise parent tries to score only one point at a time instead of taking part in a conversation that wanders in and out of several different topics.

Alice is a skillful confronter in her discussions with her son Terry, age 16. Alice helps Terry financially because he is in school and unemployed. Terry would like unlimited income, but

Alice can only afford to give him $20 a week on Monday mornings. She has reviewed the family finances with Terry, and Terry agrees that no more than $20 a week can possibly be squeezed out of the meager family budget.

Nevertheless, Terry spends his $20 on Mondays, and then hassles and nags Alice on a daily basis for more money. Alice decides to confront Terry and she wants to score a point, namely, "Talk to me about your money needs and expenses on Monday mornings only. Don't mention your money problems to me the rest of the week. I get depressed from your hassles and nagging about money." Do you see how clearly and specifically she speaks to Terry? She knows what she wants to say and says it clearly.

Terry tries to raise a lot of other points about his expenses, but Alice simply brings the conversation back to his nagging and the fact that she wants it to stop. She does listen carefully and tries to understand his points, but then she returns to the point she wants to score. Finally, as clever as Terry is, he can find no alternative but to agree to Mom's request. When Terry forgets the new deal and nags anyway, Alice simply says, "Remember our deal," and ignores him. In only a week or two, Terry sees that Mom intends to be firm about their deal, and he stops nagging.

How should adolescents speak to their parents? What is an acceptable Christian standard of conversation in the home? Richard is determined that he and his teenage daughter and son will speak to each other with courtesy, respect, and appreciation. Richard is also determined that his son and daughter will speak courteously to their mother and to their grandfather who lives with them. This whole problem of acceptable language can only be resolved by continuous confrontation, so Richard confronts the two young family members *every time* they use unacceptable speech.

He and his wife began by drawing up some basic guidelines in writing, which they revised and updated whenever necessary.

They taped these to the refrigerator door for all to see. It was a long and exhausting struggle because the daughter had a bad attitude problem, and this problem came out in her communication with her parents. So Richard persisted—and confronted whenever necessary.

The turning point came as the son and daughter saw that their parents intended to continue these confrontations until there were satisfactory results. Slowly, the sound reasoning of the parents and their patient explanations began to persuade these two young minds, and they could accept for themselves the points their parents were trying to make.

Other aspects of parent-adolescent relationships that frequently need confrontation include:

- adolescent responsibilities in the home
- habits, hygiene, eating, telling the truth
- trust versus trustworthiness: "I will trust you as you prove you are trustworthy"
- needs versus wants: "I need" usually just means "I want"
- rights versus privileges: isn't everything a privilege?
- self-control versus control by parents
- expectations of self versus expectations of others
- freedom versus responsibility

Parents are always on the right track when they confront and score points by sound reasoning.

## Use Anger to Get Results

Our adolescents need our anger at times, provided it is righteous anger. "If you are angry, do not let anger lead you into sin . . ." (Ephesians 4:26 NEB).

Anger is the complaint emotion. We must first make the complaint without anger, and if we do not gain the other person's attention and cooperation, then we are to complain a second time, only this time we use anger. Anger is a necessary, God-given emotion; we are designed to be able to express anger, and others are designed to take our anger seriously. We need to express our anger in order to let our adolescents know we are serious about our complaints.

But anger is deliberate, and it implies control. We ought to be angry, but we ought to control our tongue, fists, and feet. Our anger needs to fire us up to score points, not fuel us up to speak insults or get into a fight. A Christian parent is within bounds when expressing complaints with anger, provided his language is acceptable and he does not become abusive physically or verbally. So be emotional: let them know that you are hurting. Express anger, but control it.

## Be Assertive, Not Aggressive

There are at least three different ways to handle relationships: passively, assertively, and aggressively. All three life-styles are acceptable and appropriate at times, but the assertive life-style is very helpful in parenting teenagers. If you are passive, your adolescents will walk all over you, and if you are aggressive too often, they will walk away and not come back. With the assertive life-style, however, confrontation presses teens to consider our points, but they are not thrown on the defensive. The assertive confrontation does not turn into a fight.

Study these three approaches:

| PASSIVE | ASSERTIVE | AGGRESSIVE |
|---|---|---|
| avoiding | facing fairly | pushing |
| giving up | persisting | overwhelming |
| backing down | talking | fighting |
| accepting a settlement that is less than a fair share | holding out for a fair settlement or fifty-fifty | wanting a settlement that involves more than a fair share |
| not speaking up, giving in, throwing in the towel | bargaining, negotiating, compromising, making trade-offs | harassing, badgering, abusing and dominating |

Confront your teen assertively. To be assertive means to stand up to people, and to insist on our rights without putting others on the defensive. Assertive behavior is for conflict situations. If there is no conflict, then it is appropriate to be passive at times, and at other times a touch of aggression can spice up a relationship.

Omit blame and fault-finding. Focus on a search for solutions. Blame and fault-finding are aggressive acts which focus on the past, while the real issue is not the past but the changes we want now in the relationship.

## Be Authoritative, Not Authoritarian

Dr. Diana Baumrind has studied styles of parenting and the way children and adolescents respond to various styles of parenting. In an article published in *Child Development* in 1966, Dr. Baumrind described three main types of parents:

1. *Authoritarian Parents*—These parents are concerned about curbing self-will, and they favor punitive, forceful measures to curb the adolescent's self-will whenever the parent and teenager

disagree. These parents try to shape and control their adolescents by molding them into their own image of a person. They value obedience and conformity, and they do not encourage verbal give-and-take, believing that the teen should simply accept their word as right.

2. *Authoritative Parents*—These parents attempt to direct their adolescents' activities but in a rational, issue-oriented manner. They seek not to curb self-will but to develop it so that their teens learn to develop self-control and sound judgment. They value both self-will and disciplined conformity. They exert firm control but they want the teen to know the reasons behind their policies. They encourage verbal give-and-take because this gives them the best opportunity to make the strongest possible case for family values and standards. They use reason as well as power to exert control.

3. *Permissive Parents*—These parents are concerned that excessive controls on their teens will cause loss of control and rebellion. They make few demands for household responsibilities. They make minimal demands for orderly behavior. They present themselves to their adolescents, not as active agents responsible for shaping or controlling their future behavior, but merely as a resource for them to use as they wish. They allow the teen to regulate his own activities as much as possible; they avoid the exercise of control, and they do not encourage the adolescent to obey externally defined standards.

Baumrind found that the *authoritative* parents raised adolescents who were more self-reliant, more self-controlled, and more content. The authoritarian parents raised teens who were discontented, distrustful, and withdrawn. The permissive parents raised adolescents who were the least self-reliant and the least self-controlled. These illuminating research findings are valuable for us as we consider confrontation. *Confront authoritatively;* that is the message. Avoid the authoritarian approach and don't be permissive.

## Don't Be Afraid to Make the First Move

Confrontation means you must make the first move. You don't wait forever; you think the issue through, and you confront. If you are waiting for perfect conditions before confronting, they may never come.

*Step One.* Tell your adolescent—briefly—your complaint and how you want the complaint resolved. Don't lecture for ten minutes; the time for lectures is past. Just make the shortest possible statement on what is bothering you and propose a clear and simple solution.

*Step Two.* Listen to your adolescent's response. Think—and keep your mouth shut. You are not learning anything as long as you are doing the talking; so listen, think, and try to understand. Listen for objections to your proposal. Listen for a counter-proposal.

*Step Three.* Steps one and three are identical. No matter what your adolescent has said, repeat your own complaint and proposal. Repetition is the great clarifier, so when you repeat step one, you increase the probability that your teen understands your complaint and proposal.

*Step Four.* This step is still the parent's turn. Steps Three and Four are both up to you. In this step you try to repeat your teen's counter-proposal in order to give him or her the opportunity to clarify his statements.

**Step Five.** Summarize how far apart your proposal and your adolescent's counter-proposal are. Then, bargain, negotiate, haggle (not hassle) and compromise until you reach a mutually acceptable solution.

## General Guidelines

1. *Never* accept a solution that you believe is unfair to yourself. As long as the proposal is unfair, keep the door open by explaining repeatedly why you believe *your* proposal is more fair and why it should be accepted.
2. *Never* be in a hurry to reach a solution. Time is on the side of the one who can wait it out. As long as you are unsatisfied with your adolescent's best offer, keep on bargaining and negotiating.
3. *No deal!* You or your teen may have to let a day or even a week go by without coming to an agreement. "No deal" is always better than a "bad deal." Be patient and keep on confronting and negotiating and never be intimidated by their anger and threats.

## Teach Them How to Confront—By Your Example

Make your confrontations a learning experience for your adolescent.

***Always confront fairly, even when they are unfair.*** By your example let them learn that the conflicts and problems of family life can be resolved fairly. Project an image of yourself as a person who only wants *a fair deal,* and fair means fifty-fifty. Their goal may be unfair—meaning twenty-five to seventy-five in their favor—but you only want your fair share, and you don't intend to settle for less.

***Criticize constructively.*** Let them learn from your example how to criticize constructively. This means that all criticisms are helpful and encouraging because they point to possible improvement and solutions. Destructive criticism focuses on what is wrong and does not offer a solution.

***Be sure to revise your own proposal and make compromises.***
That is, whenever you believe your adolescent is making a valid point. Your false pride and stubbornness need to be set aside in healthy confrontations. Do not force your teen to do all the compromising unless you are very sure that his proposal is way off base. The finest parents in the world admit from time to time that their adolescents are right about a particular point, and then these parents revise their proposal accordingly.

## What Family Standards Are Non-negotiable?

There is a whole class of requirements in family life about which parents must not negotiate. These items are not negotiable because without them families cannot even exist or function adequately. These items include the parents' acceptance of their own responsibility to provide for *the bare necessities* of the lives of their children and adolescents.

Clothing is an example. The bare necessities of clothing for adolescents include:

- plain blue jeans
- plain running shoes
- plain T-shirts
- plain underwear
- plain socks
- a plain warm winter jacket
- plain warm gloves.

These bare necessities are a teenager's right. Any clothing beyond this very skimpy wardrobe is a privilege that should be

earned. Parents have a responsibility to provide the bare necessities and no more. (This does not include any spending money,
any use of the family car, or any other "fringe" benefits of
family life.)

The second non-negotiable is the adolescent's acceptance of
his own responsibility to treat his parents with courtesy, respect,
and appreciation. The third non-negotiable is the adolescent's
acceptance of his own responsibility to honor the commitments
he makes to his parents in family negotiations.

These non-negotiable elements of family life need to be discussed as often as adolescents have difficulty with them, but they
cannot be open for negotiation. They are the very reasons families
can exist as families, so they must remain non-negotiable.

But while these items are non-negotiable, parents must be
prepared to confront concerning these items. Adolescents are
quite capable of forgetting the basic requirements of family life,
and they must then be confronted. But confrontations about
non-negotiables are quite different from ordinary confrontations.
Here there can be no compromise on the parents' part; they
simply assert what to them are the essential requirements of their
particular family, and then they explain why the family must be
this kind of family. It is acceptable for adolescents to appeal for
changes, but here the parents simply must hold on firmly to the
family's basic requirements. While punishment, withdrawal of
privileges, and loss of family benefits should not normally be a
part of confrontations over negotiable items, it is acceptable and
often wise to punish or withdraw privileges if teens are stubborn
about non-negotiable aspects of family life.

It is not uncommon for families to be shaken to the very
foundations as adolescents pursue their own identity and independence. Some teenagers, especially at age 17, simply pack
their bags and leave in a huff because they can no longer accept
their parents' requirements for family life. Sometimes the ado-

lescents are wrong, and sometimes it is the parents who are in error. Sometimes both sides are wrong, and sometimes neither side is in error; it is simply time for the teens to try their wings in solo flight. Many times these solo flights succeed, but usually they crash-land and the adolescent is suddenly more humble and amenable to reason as the family reconstitutes and tries again.

In your sincere effort to be a good Christian parent, be sure that your confrontations are powerful but fair. You may very well be driven to tearful prayer many times before the parenting task is finished.

# 10

## Release Your Teen— Lovingly

"**I**f you love something, set it free. . . ." God has made us capable of such great love for our children that the love usually lasts a lifetime. We are forever ready to help, protect, and encourage our sons and daughters—when they are children, when they are adolescents, and even when they are adults. Our love for our children even extends to their children; we feel the same concern for our grandchildren as we did when their parents were growing up at home.

Colleen, age 55, gets a phone call. Her eyes sparkle, and she squeals with delight. She has just been invited by her daughter, Joyce, to spend a week helping out with the brand-new grandson. Does she want to go and love her daughter and her new grandson for a week? Nothing could please her more! And away she goes, relishing her inclusion in this celebration of a new life, and relishing the fact that *parental love never really diminishes; it just changes its focus* and manner of expression.

But Colleen has a good memory. As she packs for the trip, she remembers what it was like when Joyce was an older adolescent nearing young adulthood. Joyce was headstrong and stubborn at 14 and 15, and by age 16, Joyce was insisting on more and more freedom. Colleen remembers her fears for Joyce's safety and her future: "What if Joyce learns bad habits that last a lifetime and ruin her life? What if Joyce makes mistakes at ages 16 and 17 and 18, and these mistakes follow her and destroy her future? What if . . .? What if . . .?

She would share these fears with her husband, Bill, and he would say, "Colleen, we love Joyce, and God loves her even more than we do. It is time to let go a little more. Joyce is right—she can handle more freedom. We will sit down with her, and we will tell her we are pleased with this, concerned about that, and we will open our hand a little more. Our love requires that we seek the best for her, so we must give her more responsibility as long as she is proving that she can handle it. We will watch closely and see how it goes, and we will saturate the whole process in prayer, believing that God's love will go with Joyce as long as we are doing our part."

What pleasure Colleen felt—mixed with fear—in the final years before Joyce left home to live on her own. The fear came to Colleen whenever Joyce made a step backward, and the pleasure came to Colleen because Joyce always seemed to make two steps forward for every step backward. Because they could see Joyce's progress, Colleen and Bill were glad they worked with her to increase her freedoms. "Freedom grows giants," they had read somewhere, and they could see the growth—the giant strides toward maturity that Joyce was taking—that proved this statement to be true.

## Love Them More Than Ever, and Set Them Free

Most teens make their bid for freedom appropriately, and most parents do let go gracefully, but if the road is rocky in your family, then use all your strength, brains, and love to persevere with your adolescent until the job is done. Jay and Bobbi swear that they have learned more about life in the five years from age 40 to 45 than they learned in the previous forty, and their teacher was their youngest son, Rob, now a few weeks short of his eighteenth birthday. Rob is not bright when it comes to school learning—he is average in math, and all other subjects are a washout. But what Rob lacks in schoolwork, he makes up for in his skills with people. Rob sizes up people well, spots their weaknesses, understands power and pressure, is a master at brinkmanship, and seems constantly on the verge of trouble with the law without ever getting picked up or even contacted by the police. He did not negotiate with Jay and Bobbi for increased freedoms. He seized his freedom in a series of measured steps, and all of his parents' efforts failed to slow him down.

Rob's deliberately planned disobedience started at the time of his sixteenth birthday, when he simply refused to live by his parents' guidelines. "He was courteous in his refusal," said Bobbi afterward. When they pressured him to promise his obedience, he would, but then he would go and do as he wished. He would abide by their rules completely while at home, but he only came home when he pleased, and he would not tell them where he had been.

The first time he was gone for a whole weekend, Jay slept on the living room floor next to the telephone, in case Rob or the police or the hospital or the morgue called. Jay was terrified for Rob's safety, he was angry about being disobeyed, he was sorrowful that he was losing the old father-child relationship, he was a little jealous of the adventure and excitement Rob was probably experiencing, and he admired Rob's determination to pursue his own freedom even at the cost of parental approval. What a cluster of emotions to experience all at once toward one person!

Look at Jay's emotions toward his son Rob:

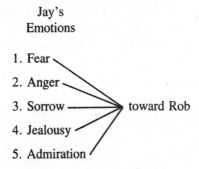

When Rob arrived home (without apology) late Sunday night, exhausted, dirty, relaxed, and content, Jay and Bobbi were beside themselves. They didn't know what to do. Rob refused to discuss where he had been and what he had been doing. He was quiet and submissive about this refusal, but would not open up. Jay and Bobbi considered all their options: punishments, grounding, loss of privileges, rewards, calling a counselor, or placing Rob in a foster home. Rob stated simply that he wanted to live at home and would keep their rules while there, but he was going to manage his own life. Jay and Bobbi pleaded, reasoned, threatened, punished, and rewarded, but Rob continued to disappear one or two weekends a month, arriving home exhausted and dirty and—you guessed it!—relaxed and content.

Jay and Bobbi contacted their pastor, professional counselors, and social agency workers for advice, and the advice amounted to this: love Rob more than ever—and set him free. Love him, warn him, advise him, listen to him, be a friend, and let him go. Understand him. This they tried to do. After two years of the strain of releasing him, Rob said to them both spontaneously, "I love you both, you know I love you. Thanks for loving me and letting go."

## Don't Love Them Too Much;
## Don't Hold Them Too Close

Linda says, "I was losing my own youth. The years were slipping by quickly, and I was bulging, sagging, graying, and slowing down. So I clamped down on my teenagers and their youthfulness, and wouldn't let them go. I could not bear to lose their laughter, their beauty, their energy. I wanted to stop the clock but they kept growing anyway, and because I couldn't let go, they left home abruptly with a tinge of bitterness and disappointment."

Gayle says, "I lost my husband after his lengthy illness. Then the twins, age 15, wanted more freedom. It was all too much for me, so I tightened my grip on them, and smothered, overprotected, meddled, interfered, and resented every bit of their happiness that didn't include me. What a good thing that they supported and encouraged each other to win their freedom! I would never have let go if they hadn't torn away."

Walt and Connie say, "We loved our two teens, but our friend told us to love them a little less and to love them at arm's length. So we backed off a little and the results were good. We never did let them go completely, but a combination of our trying to let go and the teens trying to break free did the job. We were thrilled that the kids loved us more when we let go a little. It made them try harder not to disappoint us."

Jerry says, "When Marty started to take his freedom, we didn't want him to see our tears. We were afraid they might chain him to home, so we said only that we missed him, quietly and without a fuss.

"Then, when Marty stopped phoning us as often, we didn't want him to see our anger, our frustration, and disappointment. So when he phoned, we tried to sound happy for him, and we filled the conversation with neutral questions. We didn't want our need of him to be his reason to phone home. We did everything we could to let Marty know that:

1. We were pleased with his desire to be on his own.
2. We missed him a moderate amount that did not interfere with our own happiness.
3. Our lives were moving forward without him in directions we wanted to move, and that our minds, our attention, and our concentration were focused mainly on these new directions.
4. We loved him as much as ever, but it was not a nightmare to let him go."

What problems are you having in the process of letting go? After bringing your children into this world and loving and caring for them through diapers, teething, nightmares, fevers, cuts, bruises, lunch boxes, toothaches, joys and disappointments, successes and setbacks, just how much are you hurting as they walk away? What are you saying and doing to them? Are you loving them as much as ever but showing a little less love? Or are you holding them too close?

Study the following guidelines carefully to see in what ways they may apply to you and your adolescent:

1. Don't love them too much. They need you to be loved by someone from your own generation. They need to see that your love needs are being met primarily by someone your own age or close to it. Your adolescents need to be convinced that you are not depending on them for love or for companionship. So get the rest of your life in good order so you do not *need* your teenager's love, time, and attention.

2. If your own life is not rich and full of satisfaction, be sure to try even harder to let your adolescent go. Guard against remarks and hints that appeal to their sense of pity. If you are lonely, it is your business, not theirs; so cover up your loneliness. Loneliness means only that you need a new social strategy. This

is your responsibility, not your adolescents'. They have no responsibility to enrich your social life.

When they try generously to include you in their social lives, be sure you put a limit to how much you accept their generosity. Better for you to sit at home alone and twiddle your thumbs, thinking about how to get your own life going again, than for you to look to them for love and companionship.

## You Started Letting Go the Day They Were Born

Letting go begins at birth and ends in adolescence. When your teens reach later adolescence, your hand must be fully open and they must be in full charge of their destiny. All through the three stages of their adolescence, you must be seeking ways to increase your teens' responsibility for themselves. Freedom should be thrust upon them before they demand it, as long as they are successfully handling their present measure of responsibility. Freedoms piled upon freedoms, as fast as teens can prove themselves, is the proper procedure for letting go. This means that the individual timetable of freedom depends on each adolescent. Those who handle responsibility will achieve freedom faster, while those who falter and fall must back up a little, accept a reversal of freedom, and then try again.

Maureen, age 15, is an adolescent who acts with good judgment and self-control. She deserves the freedom to manage most of her life, and her parents grant her that freedom, while carefully monitoring her progress. Maureen knows that freedom can be lost as well as gained, so she is careful to show her parents that she deserves such trust and confidence from them.

Jennifer, age 16 going on 17, is less responsible, and she has seen her freedom shrink because of irresponsible behavior. She is resentful of her recent loss of privileges, including any personal use of the family car. Her parents are tough the second time around, and Jennifer is impatient for full freedom. But two years later, when Jennifer is 18½ and legally free to come and go, she is still at home. She is there voluntarily now, though, and trying to earn by responsible behavior the many extra privileges that her parents are willing to extend if she deserves it.

Jennifer was quite shocked after her eighteenth birthday, when her parents said calmly and firmly, "Sorry, Jen, but if you choose to continue to live in our house, then you must live by our rules. You are welcome to leave if that is your choice, and you are welcome to stay if you abide by the house rules. It is up to you."

Parents must thrust new freedoms upon adolescents, but exercise discernment to be sure that they are ready for them. Always refuse new freedoms if there is evidence to suggest that the teenager needs a little more time at the present level. But remember, too, that time is running out! Plan to let go *before* their legal age of majority, so that you have some control to help them with their new freedoms.

## Your Finest Hour as a Parent

The late Dr. Haim Ginott, in his outstanding book *Between Parent and Teenager,* challenged parents to let go and make this their finest hour, their finest act of parenting. Are you letting go? Is this your finest hour? Are you listening to your reason as it tells you to let go, or are you listening to your heart as it tells you to hang on? Do not listen to your heart this time.

You deserve a heap of praise for persevering in love through all the years of your son's or daughter's childhood and adolescence. Now, finish off this good work with a touch of the best that is in you, and release your teen step-by-step into freedom. "If you love something, set it free," and go right on loving it forever. But first, set it free.

## The Test: Freedom to Make Mistakes

Teens need, in later adolescence, the freedom to make mistakes. Let them make them, and let them take full responsibility for their mistakes.

**Give them** *time-freedom.* This is freedom to use their time as they wish, wisely or foolishly. Make your teens totally responsible for getting themselves up in the morning. This means you must let them be late for school, late for work, late for breakfast, late for a shower, late for whatever. Do not wake them up. Do not call them once to get up. Do not call them twice. Time is now their responsibility. Other time responsibilities include:

- deciding when to go to bed
- deciding when to get home
- deciding when to wash
- deciding when to study
- deciding when to work

Now we are applying in detail the principles that we have been discussing. *You do not give freedom* (including time-freedom) *all at once.* Rather, you set up a *schedule of gradually increased freedoms.* This way you can see how they are handling time, and you give them more and more time-freedom as they show they can handle it. Give only one new time-freedom at a time, and then coach and encourage them to be successful in handling that new freedom. When they are successful with one freedom, add another.

**Give them** *money-freedom.* This is freedom to use their money as they wish—saving, spending, wasting, or whatever. This includes their own income from their employment, and it includes money earned within the family. Do not give teens an allowance; rather, give them wages for specific household and family chores. Always aim to get your adolescent to assume total responsibility for his own budgeting, saving, and planning for future expenses. He should have the responsibility to buy clothing and save for a trip, but he also must have the right to waste his money on junk food (many adolescents eat themselves into poverty on a regular basis), or spend all his funds on video games, pinball, or whatever. Then, when he is broke and desperate for an advance or a loan, you have the opportunity and responsibility to teach by using the most beautiful word in the English language—NO! As with all forms of freedom, you will want to extend money-freedoms gradually, teaching as you go.

**Give them *habit-freedom*.**  This is a frightening prospect for parents. We all want our adolescents to learn good habits, but they must have the right in later adolescence to make mistakes about bad habits, including lying, stealing, bad attitudes, temper outbursts, violence, laziness, sexual promiscuity, reckless driving, alcohol and drug abuse, smoking, and criminal activity of all kinds. This list is a horror and a nightmare, but it is the reality of modern adolescent options.

As their parents we have tried, all the years of their lives, to lead them toward maturity, goodness, and wisdom. Now we must extend to them the right to decide for themselves what kind of person each will become. We release them and they decide. We will continue to set a good example. *We also have the right to decide which of their habits are acceptable to us in our own house, in our own car, and in our own presence.* But what they do in their own house or someone else's house or car is up to them. We may encourage them in godliness and so we should, but we have run out of time and we no longer have the right to forbid them from evil, wickedness, sin, or any habits that we find to be personally unacceptable. Are you giving them, in later adolescence, the freedom to make mistakes?

Along with the adolescent right to make mistakes is the parental right to let teenagers take the full force of the consequences of those mistakes. *Let them suffer.* Pain is character-building. Sorrow and frustrations are essential to help teens see reality. It's fine for you to suffer with them if you insist, but do not relieve them of *their* suffering *or they will never learn.* Let them lose because of their mistakes—lose a friend, lose a year of schooling, lose their reputation, lose their self-confidence, lose their self-respect. All of these losses are part of the slide downhill, and many adolescents and young adults only come to their senses when they hit bottom.

The bottom is a great place to start (the only option, really) if that is where you are. Do not push them to the bottom; that is not fair. But if they are speeding downhill, the bottom is a great place to land to get rid of illusions of grandeur and omnipotence. At the bottom we can see more clearly, we can pick up the pieces, and we can get our lives going again. Do you have the moral strength of character to be firm, tough, and determined when they come and try to get you to bail them out?

## Help Them Break the Emotional Tie

Release your teens emotionally. Let them know in clear and simple terms that you want them to be emotionally free, not emotionally dependent. Emotional freedom means that they are:

1. free from the need of parental love;
2. free from the need of parental approval;
3. free from the fear of parental rejection.

*Emotional freedom*—what a delight! They still enjoy their parents' love, but they are not chained by it. *Emotional bond-*

*age*—what a horror! They do not feel free to make peers the significant others in their lives. What a burden and what an interference in the forward emotional development of adolescents.

Nature is helping your adolescents to break the tie of emotional dependence upon parents, but parents must help nature:

1. *By allowing adolescents to develop and pursue peer relationships.* Remember that peers must gradually replace parents as the main focus of a teenager's social and emotional life. The balance between parents and peers must shift further and further in favor of peers. Parents never will be removed from the picture entirely by well-adjusted adolescents, but well-adjusted teens break the emotional tie successfully, and they gradually make peer attachments stronger and more dominant.

2. *By refusing to let them lean on us as much* during their times of emotional upheaval. This is like weaning time down on the farm when the cows nudge away their half-grown calves and force them to forage for themselves.

3. *By developing our own new interests and new responsibilities* that make us less available to our teens. This is like the mother grizzly who keeps on wandering away from her cubs in order to pursue her own new life-interests. Finally the cubs take the hint and get on with their own lives.

You must help and encourage your teens in the pursuit of their own freedom, and this may be very difficult for you to do. You love them so much that it hurts, but resist the urge to hold them close too often. *Let them stand there alone.* Let them hurt alone; do not rush in to comfort them. Let them develop the habit of looking to peers for comfort. You may think that the peers they choose are not strong enough to be of comfort, and seeing two adolescents comfort each other may appear to you like the blind leading the blind, but keep your opinion to yourself. Remember that you need to be put in the place of lesser importance, and their future need of you for emotional support will be for emergencies only.

## Nudge Them Out of the Nest

Here we are not talking about early or middle adolescents; we are talking about later adolescents who are approaching, or have passed, the legal age of majority. Roughly speaking, ages 17, 18, and 19 are acceptable ages for leaving the nest, depending on the individual maturity of each teen.

Robert, age 17, is employed full-time. His parents charge him the full rate for room and board as a way of nudging him to the edge of the nest. They also tell him, at times affectionately and at other times matter-of-factly, that he has their approval to move out whenever he wishes to do so. He no longer has the use of the family car; this is another nudge. He is managing his own life, coming and going as he pleases, which meets his parents' approval. Laundry is the next nudge parents will use, and he will do his own laundry if he stays home much longer. He knows he *can* stay at home, and he knows he will not be shoved out. Shoved, no; but nudged, yes!

Adrienne, age 18, really needs to be living on her own so that her illusions about her "rights" can come to an end. Her father is openly suggesting to her that she try to find her own place. Brother, age 16, agrees with Father, and also pushes Sis to "move out into the big world." Mother is passive, a softie who allows herself to be exploited by Adrienne; so Adrienne says to herself, "I've got a good thing going for me with Mom as my maidservant and banker. I'll stick around home for a long time yet."

Finally the family unites against Adrienne because of her attitudes and her unfair expectations, and they effectively remove the advantages for her to stay at home. Adrienne moves out in a huff of arrogance and contempt, but soon her illusions about finding other easy marks like Mother are broken. She continues to live on her own, but appreciates her family more than she ever did before.

Nudge them out of the nest. Shoving them out should be avoided if possible, but it is sometimes necessary. A better way is to remove the financial benefits of home by charging room and board. Then remove the extra free services, such as laundry and the use of the car. It is likely that your teen will get the hint.

## Adolescents Are Superior Survivors

Release your teens because they are good survivors. They can run faster, toward trouble or away from it. They are stronger, tougher, more flexible. They fall and land on their feet. They are not sticky like flypaper, so yesterday's heartaches and disappointments are soon forgotten. They don't need your advice as much as you imagine. They need the harshness of reality and will become more realistic when you release them. They can break bad habits more easily than you think. Their mistakes will not ruin their future, and you will be pleasantly surprised that they can muddle their way along without incurring any permanent damage to mind or body, except in a very small minority of cases. They need freedom, not parents; so release them.

## A Listener, Not an Advisor, Be

A paradox of life: "We get too soon old, and too late smart." Just as parents are getting wise (sometime after age 35) and are finally figuring out God's plan and purposes for human growth and development, teens need to start figuring things out for themselves. When we are at last able to give better advice, our teens need us to be listeners. They need to think, experiment, and learn the hard way, just when our advice could save them tears and frustration. Later adolescence is the time for teens to learn on their own. Therefore, bite your tongue and a listener, not an advisor, be.

Now is the time to listen and pray. Nature challenges adolescents to become independent by means of reverse identification, which is a resistance to parental advice. Others could say the same thing as parents do, and teens would think it was fine. But if parents make the same comments, there is resistance. Therefore, be a wise parent and let your words be few. Wise people have less to say. They know more, but they talk less. They wait before they warn. They think before they suggest. Parents need to say less and make every word count more.

## Privacy Is One Step Toward Freedom

Michael, age 16, has his bedroom in the basement, and his motive for a basement bedroom is privacy. But when he put a strong lock on the door, his father removed door and all. Father was right in this case, because Michael was hiding illicit drugs in his bedroom.

Adolescents do need privacy. They need a private space and private possessions. Privacy is one step toward freedom, and wise parents encourage their teenager's privacy. But privacy must always be balanced by the parents' right to monitor what comes into their house: drugs, firearms, weapons, and pornography are examples of items about which parents have a choice, and this choice has priority over your teen's need for privacy.

Nevertheless, are you allowing your adolescent privacy as a part of your plan to release him gradually to the private pursuit of his own life? Again, this is a very difficult thing to do, so subdue your fears, and open your hand a little more.

## Err on the Early Side, But Not Too Early

Don't release adolescents too early or too late. Use your best judgment, make allowances for their individuality, and regularly increase their freedom, based on their handling of the freedoms you have already given them. They should always have as much freedom and responsibility as they can handle well, even if they are feeling the heaviness of that responsibility.

Wise parents heap on the added responsibilities appropriately. The goal is to give teenagers full freedom as soon as they can handle it. But the person who grants freedom (in this situation, it is the parent) has the power to remove it. Parents grant these freedoms, and parents can withdraw them if the withdrawal occurs well before the age of majority.

If you are not sure about adding more freedoms, proceed with caution. But if you must err, err on the early side. Many parents err in giving freedoms too late, but it is usually not an error to give freedom early, provided parents monitor the situation closely and proceed on a step-by-step basis. You will encourage teenagers to give their best effort when you trust them one step further because they proved themselves on the last step. They want to succeed and they want to be free, so keep on trying to release them further. When they fail to handle freedoms well, talk it over with them. See why it all went wrong. Make adjustments and then have a brief cooling off period with fewer freedoms. The next step is to try again. The second, third, or fourth time you try them with the same freedom, coaching as you go, they will succeed. The risk of trying over and over will have been worth it.

## It Hurts for a While, and Then—What a Relief!

Many parents sweat blood over the dangers involved in releasing their adolescents. They play the "What if . . .?"

game, and they try to look ahead and see the worst in order to give one more last warning to their teenager. They are so much into the rut—the habit—of the automatic parenting response, that they just can't seem to stop. Yet the day has come when they must view parenting as a habit to be broken, and humans only break habits by good strategy and a lot of willpower.

Why is it so difficult to stop the parenting habit? Because it hurts to let go. We always hurt when we try to break habits. Many parents experience severe emotional discomfort as they try to wean themselves of the parenting habit. But the habit must be broken, and the emotional pain of releasing adolescents is unavoidable, though temporary. "It only hurts for a little while" is the title of a love song, and this thought applies to parents too. The hurt of releasing our teens, the hurt of losing them, the hurt of missing them, the hurt of the fear for their safety, last only for a season. Then what a relief it is to be able to pursue revised goals, new interests, and new responsibilities that are worthy of the investment of the rest of our lives.

# PART FOUR

## Enjoy Them

# 11

## An Overview: Enjoy Your Teen— Frequently

Adolescence is not a mistake, it is a perfection. The Great Creator has done it perfectly, with infinite wisdom and unlimited power. He has designed adolescence as an ideal final stage of preparation for adulthood. Put in strongest terms, each biological and psychological feature of the teen years is part of God's design and is a perfect means to bring the teenager to full adulthood.

Much of the parent-adolescent conflict is related to the frustrating fact that the human genitals mature ten years before the human brain. Is this strange fact also God's creative work? If so, why? Yes, God has planned it this way so that teens will have the hormones to pursue aggressively their emotional independence. Parents want to hang on too long, and they often want to treat their teenagers like children. But this is not God's will, so He helps adolescents in their pursuit of independence.

Much of the sudden, dramatic maturity of male adolescents at age 19½, and female adolescents at age 17½, is due to a major reduction in hormone levels, and again this is part of God's perfect, creative work. Once independence is achieved at the end of the teen years, why keep the hormone level high? God's hand, even in our later adolescence, is still at the helm.

God is also in control of the psychological development of teenagers. The adolescent mind must focus on its own identity, and God has given teens a necessary preoccupation with their own identity and their own thoughts. Slowly and surely, adolescents learn how to think and reason about ideas and principles, especially ideas about being a person, and about being a partner in close relationships.

Adolescence in the majority of instances is a stunningly successful period that starts with a childlike mind and proceeds toward maturity, wisdom, and a balanced concept of self.

Through much of these years of rapid growth, teens have a supersensitivity to the opinions of their parents. They do not want to believe what their parents say. Their touchiness to parental pressure becomes extreme, but this touchiness is another useful way for them to break the tie with parents. Again, God is helping them to become persons in their own right and to break the tie of emotional dependence upon parents.

There will be a few dark days in every parent-adolescent relationship, when parent or teen is hurt, frustrated, or confused by the actions of the other. Understanding and appropriate help by parents will keep these dark days to a minimum.

Are you enjoying your teen? Keep in mind that adolescence is part of God's creative work, and this understanding will help you to enjoy your adolescent more.

## Stop Treating Them Like Children

If you want to enjoy your teens more, let reality guide you to treat them the way they are: not as children, and not as adults, but as adolescents. They are now old enough, smart enough, and strong enough to assume major responsibilities for their own care. So heap the responsibilities on them, and then coach and counsel them so that they will shoulder these responsibilities successfully.

Responsibilities are the best possible preparation for freedom. As you give your teen responsibility for managing his time, money, relationships, and duties, you are giving him the best possible preparation for the days when he leaves home.

Remember that responsibility must allow for the possibility of mistakes and failures. Adolescents sometimes learn better from mistakes and their consequences than they learn from lectures. So let them make mistakes and be sure they suffer the full consequences. They will love you later for letting them get their ego bruised.

## Who Am I?

This is the major question on the adolescent's mind. They ask themselves this question because they honestly don't know the answer.

You will enjoy your adolescent more if you understand that this question, "Who am I?", is the focus of adolescent learning. They need you to stay in the background while they search for the answers.

Remember that teenagers find their identity not just by identifying (as children do) but rather by thinking about identity. Thinking is central to adolescent learning. In order to find their identity, they must think, reason, analyze, evaluate, and compare. As children, they simply accepted and believed. Now they want evidence, reasons, facts, and sound arguments before they will change their behavior and character. Now they want to be thinkers, not merely followers who imitate others.

Not to have a clear identity is to be changeable, shifting, and unstable. Parents see these qualities in early adolescents, who appear at times to be lost in the variety of possibilities available to them. But do not despair: they will find their way and settle on their own identity. When that day comes, parents are usually surprised and delighted at the good choices that have been made.

## After Identity Comes Emotional Freedom

First, adolescents must achieve their own sense of identity, which is the focus of early adolescence. Second, teens must break the tie of emotional dependence on parents. Enjoyment of your adolescent depends on your understanding and acceptance of these two essential growth stages.

What is a sure sign that parents are *NOT* reacting wisely to the adolescent need for emotional freedom? Answer: parental feelings of personal rejection. The parents react personally and try to hang on to their adolescents. They use guilt trips to try to reconstruct a *parent-child* relationship instead of accepting the looser connection of the *parent-adolescent* relationship. Most teens see through their parents' manipulations, but a few unfortunate adolescents succumb to parental pressure and go backward into emotional dependency. For these adolescents, the natural growth into emotional independence must become a negative process of struggle against parents. This parent-created battleground is no way for parents and adolescents to enjoy each other, and it often results in bitterness and confusion that may last for years, doing the teen significant emotional harm. How much better when parents let go graciously and lovingly!

## Love and Work

The twin themes of "love" and "work" are the focus of later adolescence. They do not come one after the other; rather, they develop together. Work acts as a stabilizing force to counterbalance love. Teens who have a good example of their parents' mutual love and respect are able to benefit from the great experiences of puppy love and move into a series of ever-deepening love attachments that teach them how to give and receive love.

This is the age when there must be opportunity for adolescents to be with their peers, especially opposite-sexed peers. There must be opportunity to talk to peers, to fraternize, to socialize, to laugh, to tease, to challenge, to persuade, to allure, to love. Parents must be very much in the background when teenagers pursue relationships of affection and love.

Mental intimacy—a meeting of minds—and mutual respect and admiration are the real bases of lasting love, and teens must learn that this meeting of minds or mind-bonding is essential to a truly loving relationship. Sexual expression of that love is appropriate only in the relationship of total commitment—marriage. Adolescents know this great truth intuitively, but they must let this intuition govern their early relationships. Sex comes later, because if it comes sooner, it will interfere with (and possibly prevent) that mind-bonding so essential to permanent relationships. Parents have good reason to fear the possible negative outcomes of young love, but they must back off and let their adolescents learn.

Meaningful work (including Christian service, sports, music, schoolwork, housework, child care, part-time employment, full-time employment) is an important source of satisfaction for adolescents, who feel much better about themselves when they believe they are contributing to the maintenance of their own existence. Teens want to work, but they resent being given only trivial and insignificant tasks. They want to do work that is challenging and difficult. When they are involved in meaningful work their attitude improves, and they have better judgment in matters of love. Parents who really enjoy their adolescents are skillful in getting them to work well. Do you need to help your teen work more?

## Help Your Teen

God intends for you to help your teenager, but not too much. Sometimes we must help by not helping! Adolescents must do more and more to help themselves, and parents must do less and less. Adolescents must paddle their own canoe and not have a free ride from parents. Parental help must gradually become a matter of emergency help only, and yet emergencies seem to arise frequently with teens because of the abundance of their hormones and the shortage of their practical experience.

Teenagers need to know that they have the emotional support and goodwill of their parents in emergencies, but they also need to know that parents are holding back and are reticent to help. Sink or swim or get out of the water: this stern view is the loving Christian parents' message that the dreamworld of childhood is over, and the time for responsibility for self has arrived. Adolescents must wake up, stop dreaming, take on more and more responsibility, and take the consequences when they don't.

But exceptions make the rule, and parents enrich the parent-adolescent relationship and encourage their teen when they *occasionally* give a helping hand, not because the adolescent deserves it, but because the parent wishes the help to be an act of grace and love. The key word, however, is *occasionally*. If the help is more than occasional, teens soon take it for granted, and the parents' act of love is soon interpreted as an adolescent "right."

Parents will enjoy their teenagers more if they focus on the *four kinds of helping* that have been discussed in previous chapters:

1. Teach them.
2. Accept them.
3. Confront them.
4. Release them.

## Teach Them

It is never too late to teach, and parents should continue to teach as long as teens will listen.

First, teach the four parts of character: values, beliefs, habits, and attitudes. These four critical parts of our inner self are continually bombarded by the *false* values and beliefs and *bad* habits and attitudes of the mass media and wayward peers. Parents must work hard to present sound values and true beliefs in ways that persuade their adolescents. Sexual values are a vigorous battlefield of conflict, as the mass media promote sexual immorality to sell more magazines. Parents cannot give up and give in and lose the battle by default. They must persevere and teach by example, by instruction, by correction, and by encouragement, as long as there is opportunity.

Drug abuse and alcoholism are ongoing evil habits and addictions about which parents must also teach. These evils will not go away if ignored. There is much valuable information on these two evils for parents to study and share with their adolescents.

Finally, parents should teach their teenagers to treat them like royalty—with courtesy, respect, kindness, and appreciation. Parents, you should expect to be treated well by those you have loved and helped so long, and you should refuse to accept discourtesy and lack of appreciation. Be prepared to confront your adolescents every time they display discourtesy and lack of respect for you.

## Accept — Love — Reject — Confront

You are already a long way on the road to enjoying your teenager if you understand that relationships in general, and parent-adolescent relationships in particular, need the vitality and variety that come from responding to present reality. What is the reality—moment by moment—of your parent-adolescent relationship? Do you respond to that reality? The hyphenated expression "accept-love-reject-confront" is intended to suggest that you as parents must roll with the punches and call a spade a spade in a spontaneous flow of honesty and understanding.

Teenagers need parents who care enough to "speak the truth in love," where "truth" is the parents' honest evaluation of the present state of the relationship. But it is not just "give," but rather "give-and-take," and parents must listen to their adolescent's concerns as well. Is your parent-teen relationship an open, two-way communication in which you are honest with each other? Can your adolescents speak their minds to you, and can they count on you hearing?

If you need to rejuvenate and intensify the parent-adolescent relationship by honestly speaking your mind, make it a matter of earnest prayer that God will give you eyes to see the full truth from all perspectives—God's, your teen's, and your own. Then speak the truth, first in small doses and then building up the dosage until you are frank, honest, direct, and open all of the time. Give them time to adjust to your increased honesty, though it won't take them long to be able to respond in kind.

Think about the expression "accept-love-reject-confront." Which parts of this quartet do you need to strengthen? Which parts do you need to weaken? Write out the expression and tape it to your bedroom mirror to remind you to be more open and honest in both positives and negatives. Your teens need your full verbal response to the realities of the parent-adolescent relationship.

## Release Them

Some parents say, "I'm not going to release them. I'm going to hang on until they break away. This will prevent a few heartaches and disasters, so I am justified in hanging on." But this is not God's way. Others say, "I'm going to release them soon." But for these parents, "soon" never comes.

Fortunately, most adolescents make their bid for freedom appropriately, and most parents let go graciously. Regardless, there is always risk—to life, to limb, to health, to reputation. Guarantees do not exist for all the tomorrows of your teenager's life.

Be a risk-taker. It is God's plan that you should let go. Release your teenagers lovingly and welcome them if they have to return occasionally to the nest during their adjustment to freedom. Help them (sparingly) if they need a helping hand during an emergency. Love them, and let them go again, and again, and again.

## Enjoy Them

Do not try to enjoy your teen. Joy is not something you try to obtain; *joy can only be earned* by right actions. Therefore, act rightly toward your teenager, and in time you will enjoy your adolescent.

Joy only comes as a reward for a job well done. Whenever we sense that we are handling the parent-adolescent relationship wisely, we will experience joy. That is a promise from God's Word. If you want joy (Philippians 4:4), you must think and act rightly (thoughts and actions that are "true," "noble," "just," "excellent," and "admirable"—study Philippians 4:8 NEB).

Your joy will come in the parent-teen relationship when you really do *understand* them and when you *help* them in a wise and appropriate manner. These two great actions—understanding and helping—are the key to enjoying your teen. Understand and help wisely, and the joy will be yours.